RECLAIMING
THE SIXTH
AMENDMENT

How the Structure of the Criminal Justice System Recognizes the Right to Counsel but Never Enforces It

Freya D. Pearson

ISBN: 979-8-218-91667-1

Printed in the United States of America

First edition.

Website: finalityisnotjustice.com
Contact: freya@finalityisnotjustice.com

Contents

Introduction

This book is not an accusation against individual judges, prosecutors, or defense counsel. It is an examination of a system that repeatedly allows integrity to speak, but never allows it to decide.

What follows is not a claim that constitutional standards have changed. They have not. The language of the Sixth Amendment remains intact. The laws governing effective assistance of counsel, harmless error, prejudice, and deference remain firmly in place. What has changed is how those standards are applied, and more importantly, how that application is insulated from meaningful scrutiny.

Courts routinely acknowledge the difficulty of indigent defense. That acknowledgment rarely translates into enforcement. Instead, it becomes the rationale for restraint. Performance failures are reframed as strategy. Omissions are explained as discretion. Silence is treated as intentional choice. In this way, constitutional compliance is declared complete without the court ever examining whether the right functioned in practice.

This book examines how that declaration is produced.

It traces how structural laws and procedures that are designed to safeguard defendants are routinely transformed into mechanisms that protect outcomes. Harmless error review becomes a substitute for jury fact-finding. Deference replaces adversarial testing. Ineffectiveness review demands proof while denying access to the very materials necessary to establish it. At each stage, responsibility quietly shifts away from the system and onto the defendant, who is often proceeding pro se, after counsel has withdrawn, on a record already fixed against them.

This is not a book about bad actors. It is a book about structural permission.

When courts accept restraint from defense counsel as benign in one moment while presuming vigor in all others, they sever posture from practice, and constitutional review becomes an exercise in abstraction rather than examination.

The result is not error corrected, but error absorbed. But, it is error.

These patterns do not arise from misunderstanding. They persist because the system is designed to normalize them. Appellate review substitutes judicial reconstruction for adversarial testing. Post-conviction review demands proof while denying discovery. Parallel proceedings are treated as unrelated even when they directly affect the criminal case. Each court disclaims responsibility for the whole, while collectively ensuring that no remedy emerges.

Makes one ponder: What happens when all of these accepted legal procedures interact with each other, repeatedly, across stages, with the same institutional incentives driving them?

Readers may notice that as the analysis moves through different structures, standards, and procedural stages, the path begins to feel familiar. That repetition is not incidental. It is the structure revealing itself. Whether the court speaks in the language of discretion, deference, harmlessness, waiver, or strategy, the destination remains the same. Each law, as articulated in theory, yet each resolves the inquiry in an identical way. The defendant enters through different constitutional doors only to arrive at the same result. What changes is the vocabulary. What does not change is the outcome. This repetition is not a flaw in the argument. It is the evidence of a system designed to process claims without ever allowing them to alter the result.

For the defendant, this means that no matter which constitutional avenue is pursued, the structure has already decided where the path will end. It is about a system that has already decided the outcome before the argument even begins.

I do not claim to offer easy solutions. I do claim that the questions raised here can no longer be dismissed as anomalous, personal, or rare. They have become structural. Until they are acknowledged as such, the promise of the Sixth Amendment will remain exactly that.

A promise, unkept.

Chapter 1
The Right That Exists on Paper

A Right Declared and Assumed

The Sixth Amendment promises more than representation. It promises a meaningful defense. Yet over time, the criminal justice system has come to treat the mere appointment of counsel as fulfilling that promise, rather than its beginning.

The question is two-fold: whether the right was ever meaningfully enforced, and how the system has chosen to define what is meaningful.

That distinction matters because constitutional rights are not self-executing. They require mechanisms that ensure compliance, accountability, and correction when violations occur. Without such mechanisms, a right can exist fully articulated in law while lacking functionality in practice.

The Sixth Amendment survives in modern practice not because it is enforced, but because it is assumed, by appointment and procedural completion. Appointment and completion stand in for performance. From that point on, the right is presumed to have functioned. Inquiry stops. Enforcement becomes unnecessary. The right does not disappear. It becomes administratively invisible.

This displacement stabilizes outcomes. Appellate courts inherit records presumed adequate. Oversight bodies encounter finality rather than failure. Administrative systems rely on closure as legitimacy. Each institution encounters a right that has already been declared satisfied by the time it arrives.

The post-Gideon landscape illustrates this dynamic with particular clarity. The right to counsel was formalized, universalized, and celebrated. What was never formalized was a corresponding obligation to verify that the right operated as intended. Appointment became the endpoint of constitutional concern. The right was secured in theory and hollowed in practice without ever being repudiated.

In our system, a right that must be enforced creates friction. A right that is presumed satisfied creates order.

When Presence Is Mistaken for Protection

The federal system reflects this contradiction across every circuit and at every stage of review. Representation is guaranteed, but enforcement is treated as complete by default and tolerates no challenge. Counsel effectiveness is constitutionally required, yet diluted by an unwritten judicial accommodation that treats scarcity, workload, and institutional strain as justification for reduced scrutiny.

Courts routinely acknowledge the difficulty of indigent defense. That acknowledgment rarely translates into enforcement. Instead, it becomes the rationale for deference. Performance failures are re-framed as strategy. Omissions are explained as discretion. Silence is treated as intentional choice. In this way, constitutional compliance is declared complete without the court ever examining whether the right functioned in practice.

The burden then shifts. Defendants must demonstrate failure they could not see, prevent, or correct. They are required to prove preju-dice caused by omissions that never entered the record. Meanwhile, counsel's explanations are accepted without contemporaneous test-ing. What is called neutrality operates as asymmetry.

Presence becomes protection by declaration. The courtroom appears adversarial. The docket reflects representation. The Constitution is cited. Inquiry stops.

Efficiency Elevated Over Constitutional Function

Trial courts are tasked with managing cases efficiently. That man-date shapes everything that follows. Speed is rewarded. Closure is praised. Finality is treated as competence.

In this environment, the mere presence of counsel is treated as proof of fairness. Serious failures in representation go unexamined so long as proceedings move forward and the record appears orderly. The question shifts from whether the Sixth Amendment was honored to whether it was procedurally satisfied.

Post-conviction review is offered as the corrective, yet it arrives only after liberty has been taken and institutional positions have hardened. Those claims return to the same courts that accepted the original proceedings. The same Judges are asked to review conduct that they previously observed and approved. This structure is not incidental. It is by design.

How Procedure Absorbs Constitutional Failure

Once enforcement is displaced, procedure absorbs what remains. Preservation laws determine what may be heard. Forfeiture laws determine what may be considered. Harmless error doctrines determine what may be ignored.

Each standard appears reasonable in isolation. Together, they create a system calibrated to contain constitutional failure rather than confront and correct it.

If objections were not raised, claims are forfeited. If issues were not preserved, review is denied. If harm cannot be quantified, error is deemed harmless. At each stage, the focus moves further from enforcement and closer to closure. While the burden of those failures now rest with the defendant.

This produces predictable results. Violations are segmented, failures are minimized, and structural breakdown is reclassified as nonprejudicial conduct. Reduced to questions of degree rather than kind, even profound breakdowns lead to judges debating over whether counsel slept long enough during a defendant's trial to matter. That such questions are entertained at all, reveals the system's orientation.

Over time, violations stop registering as violations. They become background conditions of practice, normalizing constitutional failure rather than correcting it.

The Sixth Amendment as Certification, Not Constraint

In this context, the Sixth Amendment functions as certification rather than constraint. It confirms that a procedural requirement was met, not that a constitutional safeguard operated.

The presence of counsel certifies fairness even when independence, preparation, and adversarial testing are absent, and even when counsel lacks the knowledge, experience, or positioning necessary to identify, investigate, or pursue an actual defense. The right is treated as proof of legitimacy rather than a demand for scrutiny.

Certification satisfies institutions. Constraint disrupts them. The system chooses certification.

Judicial Deference as an Operating Principle

Judicial deference is often described as restraint. In practice, it functions as insulation. Courts regularly defer to defense counsel's decisions, explanations, and silence, even when those choices directly affect the constitutional rights of the accused. This deference is not neutral. It operates asymmetrically, shielding professional actors while imposing procedural consequences on defendants.

In the trial setting, judicial action is not automatic. Courts do not search for constitutional failure. They wait to be moved. Objections must be raised. Motions must be filed. Arguments must be pressed. Absent that activation, the court proceeds as though nothing requires intervention.

When counsel is ineffective at the moments that matter most, the silence that follows does not register as a warning. It resolves the issue. The absence of objection is treated as acquiescence, the failure to move the court as strategic choice. In that moment, constitutional protection evaporates, not because it has been denied, but because it has never been invoked.

This is the structural trap. The right to counsel is enforced only if counsel performs well enough to demand enforcement. When counsel lacks the knowledge, experience, or capacity to act, the system treats that incapacity as consent. In that structure, the Sixth Amendment is enforced only if counsel performs well enough to trigger enforcement. Failure is not corrected. It is normalized. And by the time the consequences are visible, the moment for intervention has already passed.

That silence is not merely overlooked. It is later converted into law. Preservation law treats the failure to object as forfeiture. Waiver doctrine treats inaction as intentional relinquishment. Harmless-error analysis treats unchallenged violations as inconsequential. Strickland's prejudice requirement converts trial-level incapacity into post hoc speculation. Each operates independently. Together, they ensure that what went unchallenged when it mattered most cannot be meaningfully challenged later.

By the time review occurs, the absence of action has already been reclassified as choice, and the absence of inquiry as finality. What began as ineffective representation is transmuted into procedural default. Constitutional protections are not weighed against the failure. They are bypassed by it.

This pattern continues on appeal. Appellate courts describe themselves as courts of review, not of first instance. They rely heavily on the trial record, even when the alleged failure is the absence of something that never made it into that record. Deference to counsel's choices becomes a substitute for examination of counsel's effectiveness. What cannot be seen in the record is treated as nonexistent, even when its absence is itself the constitutional harm.

Sidestepping Sixth Amendment Protections Through Presumption and Continuity

In this structure, Sixth Amendment protections are not openly denied. They are sidestepped. Courts retain the theoretical authority to remove counsel, but the exercise of that authority is rare and treated as extraordinary. More commonly, counsel remains in place and proceeds unchanged. Where a defendant lacks the legal knowledge or capacity to articulate the nature of counsel's failure with procedural specificity, that inability is not treated as evidence of vulnerability. It is treated as absence of error. The burden of identifying ineffective representation thus falls on the very person least equipped to carry it, and silence or imprecision is converted into confirmation that no failure occurred.

That failure does not end with the individual case. When ineffective representation is neither identified nor addressed, it carries forward. Counsel moves on to the next indigent defendant without any intervening evaluation of performance, without remedial action, and without institutional acknowledgment that anything went wrong. So moving forward, defendants who lack the legal knowledge or experience to recognize ineffective assistance are left unprotected, and the system treats their silence as confirmation that representation was adequate. The defendant knows that something is wrong, but lacks the ability to properly articulate it.

The result is a sustained presumption of readiness untethered from demonstrated performance. Counsel is presumed prepared for trial not because preparation has been shown, but because no mechanism exists to test it. Objective indicators that would otherwise prompt concern are disregarded. Extreme caseloads, chronic plea resolution, and extended periods without a single trial are treated as ordinary features of practice rather than warning signs of diminished adversarial capacity.

For example, counsel may handle more than four hundred cases over a five-year period without taking a single case to trial, a statistical impossibility that does not even prompt judicial inquiry, intervention, or review. The court instead treats that record as evidence of competent representation.

The system proceeds on the fiction that trial competence cannot erode through disuse, and therefore refuses to examine whether it has. That presumption rests on an even deeper one: that counsel possessed meaningful trial competence to begin with. In many cases, that premise is never tested at all.

What the system preserves in this posture is not the Sixth Amendment guarantee, but the uninterrupted movement of cases. Ineffective representation does not trigger intervention. It is permitted to recur, uncorrected, from one defendant to the next, insulated by presumption, deference, and the absence of inquiry.

In the end, Sixth Amendment protection is conditioned not on whether a defense was provided, but on whether a defendant is capable of proving its absence within a system designed not to actually look.

Why Structural Failure Rarely Appears as Error

Structural failure does not announce itself as error within a system that defines compliance procedurally. Error is measured by deviation from prescribed steps, not by whether constitutional protections functioned in fact. When the correct forms are filed, the appropriate appearances made, and the required actors present, the system records success even when the underlying ineffective counsel has failed completely.

This setup renders constitutional breakdown largely invisible. Failures that occur through omission rather than commission do not register as error at all. The absence of investigation, the failure to challenge evidence, the failure to test the government's case, or the failure to prepare for trial are not treated as discrete events subject to review. They are absorbed into the background of professional judgment and presumed strategy. What is never done cannot easily be identified as error because it leaves no procedural footprint.

Structural failure is further obscured by fragmentation. Responsibility is dispersed across stages, actors, and structures, such that no single decision point appears reviewable in isolation. Trial courts rely on counsel to perform. Appellate courts rely on the record produced below. Post-conviction courts rely on prior rulings and procedural bars. Each institution encounters only a partial picture and defers to what came before. The cumulative effect is never assessed. Harm that emerges from the interaction of these layers disappears, because it cannot be attributed to a single, reviewable act.

In this environment, legitimacy is maintained through continuity rather than correction. The system continues to operate smoothly, cases continue to move, and outcomes continue to be finalized. The absence of disruption is taken as evidence of validity. Constitutional erosion proceeds quietly, not because it is unseen, but because it does not take a form that the system is designed to recognize.

What results is a profound mismatch between constitutional promise and institutional measurement. The Sixth Amendment fails, not loudly, but silently. Its breakdown does not trigger alarm because it does not resemble error. It resembles normal operation.

Stability Without Legitimacy

The criminal justice system is stable. Cases move. Judgments issue. Appeals conclude. That stability is not accidental. It is produced through a system that confines constitutional inquiry to procedural compliance rather than constitutional function. When the required steps are completed and the appropriate actors are present, the system records success even when the defendant's constitutional rights have not functioned as protections.

Stability, however, is not legitimacy. Legitimacy requires confidence that constitutional protections function as safeguards, not merely as declarations. When enforcement is replaced by assumption, the system's claim to constitutional legitimacy becomes hollow. Rights that are always declared but rarely tested lose their meaning without ever being displaced.

Over time, the absence of disruption is mistaken for proof of legitimacy. Smooth operation becomes evidence that nothing is wrong. Finality is treated as validation. Yet the very features that produce stability also ensure that constitutional failure remains unseen and uncorrected. The system does not collapse under this arrangement. It settles into it.

What emerges is a criminal process that is orderly, predictable, and insulated from challenge, but increasingly detached from the constitutional values it claims to embody. Stability is preserved. Legitimacy is assumed. The distance between the two quietly widens.

What This Chapter Establishes

This chapter establishes a foundational distinction. The Sixth Amendment has not failed because it was misunderstood or rejected. It has failed because enforcement was never structurally built into the system responsible for applying it. Appointment of Counsel became the endpoint rather than the beginning. Procedure became the substitute for scrutiny. Deference became the mechanism of resolution. What remains is a right that exists everywhere on paper and almost nowhere in operation.

The Sixth Amendment is framed as a guarantee of representation, but its function is adversarial testing. When the system treats appointment as satisfaction rather than initiation, enforcement quietly disappears, and a right that cannot be enforced becomes indistinguishable from a right not meaningfully possessed at all.

The chapters that follow trace how this structure functions across institutions that present themselves as separate and independent. Courts, oversight bodies, and administrative systems appear to occupy distinct roles, each disclaiming responsibility for enforcement beyond its own narrow function. In practice, they do not operate independently. They function in sequence, reinforcing one another through deference, formal compliance, and institutional handoff. Each relies on the appearance of separation to justify inaction, and each passes constitutional responsibility forward without ever requiring its enforcement. What emerges is not a failure to recognize the Sixth Amendment, but a system calibrated to satisfy it on paper while denying its protections in practice.

The next chapter turns to enforcement in practice. It examines how enforcement quietly disappeared, not through repeal or open defiance, but through narrowing, procedural redirection, and the expansive use of judicial discretion. Discretion does not merely shape outcomes in this system. It distorts constitutional obligation itself, converting enforceable guarantees into optional inquiry and managerial choice. Accurate description is therefore not adversarial. It is the only means by which accountability can begin.

Chapter 2
The Architecture of Disappearing Enforcement

From Right to Remedy

This chapter explains how Sixth Amendment enforcement disappears not through repeal, hostility, or misunderstanding, but through the coordinated operation of settled legal practices. Although ineffective assistance of counsel is the primary mechanism through which the right to counsel is formally enforced, it does not operate in isolation. Its application is shaped and constrained by related procedures that govern standards of review, procedural default, harmless error, post-conviction relief, and certificates of appealability, all of which embed discretion, deference, and finality into the enforcement process.

Ineffective Assistance of Counsel and the Neutralization of Failure

The ineffective assistance of counsel is the principal mechanism through which the federal system claims to enforce the Sixth Amendment right to counsel. It is presented as a corrective safeguard, designed to identify and remedy breakdowns in representation after they occur. In practice, it functions less as a tool of enforcement than as a structure for managing when enforcement will be withheld.

This recalibration is driven by an unwritten rule that supersedes the law itself: finality. When acknowledgment of ineffective assistance would require reversal, a new trial, evidentiary development, or renewed litigation, finality prevails. Performance that might otherwise be deemed deficient is reframed as reasonable. Prejudice that would otherwise matter is dismissed as speculative. The legal standard is stretched precisely at the moment enforcement would require the proceeding to begin again.

Under ineffective assistance of counsel laws, acknowledgment of deficient performance does not trigger enforcement. It triggers a reclassification decision. The court does not ask whether counsel's failure to investigate, prepare, or meaningfully participate violated the Sixth Amendment. It asks how that same conduct should be characterized at the procedural stage in which the claim appears, whether at trial, on appeal, or in post-conviction review. The classification turns not on the severity of the failure, but on what acknowledging it as a constitutional violation would require the court to do at that point.

The ineffective assistance standard purports to measure performance against prevailing professional norms. In practice, those norms are never actually defined. Courts invoke them without identifying what competent representation requires in concrete terms. They refer to professional judgment without specifying the obligations counsel was required to meet. The standard is treated as self-evident, yet its content is left unstated.

This indeterminacy is not confined to differences between jurisdictions. The standard often shifts within the same court. Identical attorney conduct may be treated as a constitutional violation in one case and as reasonable strategy, harmless error, or procedural default in another. The distinction does not turn on the conduct itself, but on timing, posture, and the court's discretionary interest in preserving the outcome before it. The behavior does not change. The classification does.

What should be an inquiry into counsel's constitutional obligations becomes an exercise in defendant speculation. Defendants are required to reconstruct what competent representation would have required, to identify investigative steps that were never taken, and to explain why those steps were constitutionally necessary, all without a stable or articulated standard to measure against.

As a result, the same attorney conduct is evaluated differently depending on the remedy it would trigger. When enforcement would be limited, the conduct may be labeled deficient. When enforcement would be disruptive, the standard rises until the conduct no longer qualifies as a violation at all. The height of the bar is not fixed by constitutional obligation. It is adjusted to preserve finality.

This is how the right to effective assistance of counsel is displaced in practice. The written standard remains intact, but an unwritten rule governs its application. Finality supersedes enforcement. Courts replace constitutional obligation with the discretionary power to reclassify conduct so that reversal, retrial, or renewed proceedings can be avoided. The Sixth Amendment survives in language, but its remedies are subordinated to the system's refusal to reopen what it has already closed.

The Architecture of Ineffective Assistance of Counsel

Ineffective assistance of counsel rests on a two-part standard. Defendants must show deficient performance and resulting prejudice. On paper, the test appears balanced. It acknowledges that counsel can fail and that failure should matter. In operation, the structure is calibrated so that the two prongs almost never converge in a way that forces enforcement.

Deficiency is evaluated through deference rather than examination. Courts are asked to assess whether counsel's investigation, preparation, and adversarial testing were constitutionally adequate, yet they routinely rely on post hoc characterizations rather than affirmative inquiry. Strategic explanations are accepted even when unsupported. Omissions are presumed intentional. Silence is treated as choice. Performance is judged not by what was done or required, but by what courts are willing to assume.

This mode of evaluation collapses directly into discretion. Courts decide whether to interrogate counsel's explanations, whether to treat omissions as constitutionally significant, and whether to probe the adequacy of representation at all. These decisions are not compelled by constitutional standards. They are discretionary choices. What appears as deference is, in practice, a preference for assumption over examination.

The consequences are predictable. When counsel fails to investigate potential witnesses, those failures are dismissed as strategic rather than examined as breakdowns in adversarial testing. When counsel fails to obtain records, pursue expert analysis, or prepare a defense for trial, those omissions are observed and then stripped of legal consequence. Courts focus on isolated moments instead of the representation as a whole, fragmenting failure until it no longer appears actionable.

Prejudice is filtered through speculation, not inquiry. Courts ask whether the outcome would have been different absent the failure, a question posed only after the case is over, the record is closed, and the jury is gone. Judges are asked to imagine an alternative proceeding that never occurred, using a record shaped by the very deficiencies under review. Where counsel failed to investigate, there is little evidence to evaluate. Where counsel failed to prepare a defense for trial, there is no adversarial baseline for comparison. The absence created by counsel's failure becomes the justification for denying relief.

Each prong is difficult to satisfy standing alone. Together, they form a test that appears to evaluate ineffective representation while avoiding its enforcement. The Sixth Amendment grants courts wide discretion without imposing corresponding obligations to define deficiency, develop inquiry, or confront systemic failure. That discretion is routinely exercised to deny indigent defendants' relief. The result is not neutral application of law, but a structure that systematically produces denial rather than correction.

Deference as Default

Deference is not an incidental feature of ineffective assistance of counsel. It is designed as its organizing principle. Courts do not arrive at deference after examining counsel's conduct. They begin there. Counsel's performance is presumed to fall within the wide range of reasonable professional assistance, and that presumption controls the analysis from the outset. It is rarely disturbed, and it is almost never tested.

This default posture has predictable effects. Absence is converted into approval. Where the record is silent, courts resolve that silence in counsel's favor. Where counsel offers no explanation, courts supply one. Where no investigation occurred, courts presume it was unnecessary. The lack of action is treated as if it reflected a considered professional judgment entitled to respect, even when no such judgment is demonstrated.

Deference also reshapes the inquiry into an adversarial exchange between the defendant and counsel. The defendant must identify what counsel failed to do and then overcome the claim that the failure was strategic. Counsel, whose professional reputation and future work may be affected by an ineffective assistance finding, has every incentive to characterize omissions as deliberate judgment rather than neglect or breakdown. Courts routinely accept these explanations without probing their factual basis, transforming self-protective justification into a controlling narrative.

Indigent defendants are required to rebut strategic explanations offered by the very lawyer whose performance is at issue, using a record that reflects only what counsel chose to document. The defendant's inability to disprove those explanations is treated not as evidence of structural imbalance, but as confirmation that counsel acted competently.

The result is consistent. The less documented the failure, the more insulated it becomes. Silence operates as proof of adequacy. Omission is recast as intention. What should invite scrutiny instead triggers deference.

Even when a defendant establishes deficient performance, discretion does not recede. It relocates to prejudice, where courts resolve the claim through speculation rather than adjudication. The cycle continues, now under the banner of deference. Judges ask whether the outcome would have been different had counsel performed adequately, a question answered not by evidence but by prediction. In doing so, the court imagines an alternative trial that never occurred, assesses evidence that was never developed, and weighs arguments that were never made, effectively assuming a role that belongs to a jury rather than to post hoc judicial review.

Because the record reflects only what occurred under deficient representation, courts speculate that unpursued investigations would not have yielded meaningful evidence, that uncalled witnesses would not have been credible, or that unmade arguments would not have persuaded a jury. These conclusions are reached without hearings, without development, and without testing. The absence created by counsel's failure becomes the basis for concluding that the failure caused no harm.

In this way, deference operates across both prongs of the ineffective assistance of counsel test to prevent enforcement at every stage. If failure is alleged, it is deferred to strategy. If deficiency is proven, it is declared non prejudicial by speculation. At no point is the right to counsel examined in a manner that requires correction. Deference does not merely shape the analysis. It ensures the outcome.

Deference does not merely shape review. It determines whether Sixth Amendment violations will ever be adjudicated as violations at all.

How the System Describes Itself When Unguarded

The following excerpt is drawn from a recorded consultation with a court-appointed attorney.

It is reproduced in the attorney's own words.

No names are used.
No identifying dates or case details are included.

The following excerpt reproduces the attorney's words verbatim, with minor edits for clarity and removal of identifying material:

"CJA is different than retained. If you want that level, that's retained."

"I've had a lot of people convert over and say, 'Okay, I want that,' and then here's the fee. And I will turn myself inside out for you."

"On CJA, I'm going to turn myself inside out within the parameters of being court-appointed. I'm going to give you constitutionally sufficient representation. But no, we're not going to be trading emails at nine or ten at night, reading documents together, traveling, or commiserating. You're at a different level."

"It's several things. I look at it as commitment. You want every ounce of my commitment. What are you giving me? Nothing. And I'm just being honest."

"I'll do a good job. But when people find out the difference between what I do on CJA and what I do for retained clients, I wouldn't want to be on the other end of that stick."

"I set limits on CJA clients that I don't set for retained clients. That's the difference."

ANALYSIS

What stands out most is not the reference to money or even the admission of limits. It is the casualness with which the line is drawn. There is no shame, no hesitation, and no sense that what is being described is aberrational or improper. The attorney is not explaining a failure. He is explaining the rules of the system as he understands them, in the same manner one would explain office hours, billing practices, or workload boundaries.

That casualness matters. It signals normalization. The distinction between appointed and retained representation is treated not as a constitutional problem, but as an accepted feature of practice. The difference is acknowledged openly, justified without discomfort, and framed as both reasonable and inevitable.

What legal reasoning later absorbs as "strategy" or "professional judgment" appears here as an ordinary expectation about how court-appointed representation works, with structural limits later relabeled as discretion to shield the system from indigent defendants' ineffective assistance claims. The limits being described are not choices made to advance a defendant's interests. They are constraints imposed by the appointment model, recast as strategy only after the fact, to insulate the system from claims of ineffective assistance by indigent defendants.

The most revealing statement in the excerpt is the attorney's acknowledgment that he would not want to be on the receiving end of the representation that he provides in the court-appointed context. That admission is significant because it is a self-assessment rather than an accusation. It reflects an internal understanding that the representation is materially different in ways that would matter to a defendant.

If the limits described were merely differences in style or preference, there would be no reason to reject them for oneself. The statement instead confirms that the distinction is substantive. It recognizes that the level of advocacy provided under appointment is one the attorney himself would avoid if given the choice.

The governing standards do not account for this recognition. Courts presume that appointed representation satisfies constitutional requirements without asking whether those providing it believe it does. Deference is extended automatically. Competence is presumed abstractly. The lived reality of constrained advocacy is treated as irrelevant.

This is how enforcement disappears without ever being denied. Structural limitation is relabeled as discretion. Constraint is reframed as judgment. And when indigent defendants later raise claims of ineffective assistance, these same limits are invoked as evidence that counsel acted reasonably rather than as proof that the system failed to provide the conditions necessary for meaningful representation.

In one post-conviction proceeding, counsel acknowledged that he had to "watch what [he] did" to the prosecutor in order to avoid affecting his future cases. The admission was not speculative, rhetorical, or inferred. It was direct. It reflected an awareness that confrontation in the present case carried professional consequences beyond the interests of the defendant.

Standing alone, such a statement would already raise serious concerns about divided loyalty. A defense attorney's obligation is singular: to the client. The constitutional right to counsel presumes that representation will not be calibrated to protect future professional relationships, particularly with the opposing party. Yet the court did not treat the admission as a disclosure of conflicted representation. Instead, it was reframed as context-specific and benign.

The court confined the significance of the statement to the procedural moment in which it arose, characterizing it as a reasonable explanation for a tactical choice related to a scheduling extension. In doing so, the court treated the admission as though it described a narrow, isolated consideration, rather than a governing posture toward the prosecution.

This limitation was not neutral. At the time the statement was evaluated, the record already contained allegations of broader failures of representation, including the failure to meaningfully confront prosecutorial misconduct and investigative irregularities. Counsel himself had acknowledged awareness of those issues. Yet the court assessed the admission of divided loyalty as though it bore no relationship to those omissions.

By isolating the statement to a single procedural context, the court avoided the question that the record itself demanded: whether an attorney who admits moderating his conduct to preserve future prosecutorial relationships can be presumed to have exercised undivided loyalty in any aspect of the representation. That question was never answered through analysis. It was resolved through compartmentalization.

When defense counsel signals restraint to preserve future cases, that posture does not govern a single decision in isolation. It becomes an orientation that necessarily informs the court of how counsel approaches objection, investigation, confrontation, and enforcement throughout the representation. Courts nonetheless treat such admissions as context limited, severing them from the broader conduct that they explain. In doing so, they accept a fiction that counsel may fear confrontation in one moment, yet act without restraint in all others.

An attorney who fears professional retaliation over a routine scheduling matter cannot be presumed fearless when confronting prosecutorial misconduct, challenging false testimony, or insisting on enforcement of constitutional guarantees. The court cannot logically accept the existence of that concern in one context while denying its influence everywhere else.

To confine such a statement to a scheduling decision is not a neutral limitation. It is an artificial severance designed to preserve the conviction while avoiding the consequences of what the statement reveals. If the concern exists at all, it permeates the representation. Treating it as compartmentalized does not neutralize its significance, it obscures it.

The result is not merely the minimization of a troubling admission. It is the redefinition of constitutional review itself. Courts are permitted to acknowledge conflicts in theory while neutralizing them in practice by narrowing their scope until no remedy can attach. Integrity is allowed to speak, but it is never allowed to govern.

In this way, the right to counsel is formally recognized while its enforcement is displaced by deference, segmentation of the record, and post hoc rationalization. The system preserves outcomes by containing admissions rather than reckoning with their implications. What remains is not adjudication, but containment.

The excerpt does not expose misconduct. It exposes design. It shows how a right can exist formally while operating under conditions that predictably prevent it from functioning as intended, and how the legal system absorbs that reality by refusing to see it.

Prejudice as Speculation Rather Than Inquiry

The prejudice prong is often described as the safeguard that prevents trivial claims from succeeding. In practice, it functions as a fail-safe against enforcement. Where deference protects counsel's conduct from scrutiny, prejudice ensures that even clear failure rarely results in relief. Together, they close the door to correction.

Prejudice analysis asks whether there is a reasonable probability that the result would have been different. That question is posed only after the proceeding has concluded, the record has closed, and the opportunity for correction has passed. At that point, courts are no longer deciding how to protect a constitutional right. They are deciding whether to reopen a finished case. Finality quietly replaces fairness as the operative concern.

In this posture, prejudice is not examined. It is resolved through speculative determinations designed to preserve finality. Courts use the same process as it always uses, it imagines an alternative proceeding that never occurred, using a record produced by deficient representation. They weigh evidence that was never developed, testimony that was never elicited, and arguments that were never made. The inquiry does not ask what competent representation would have produced. It asks whether the absence created by failure can be declared harmless. The answer is almost always yes, not as a finding of fact, but as a condition of finality.

The burden falls entirely on the defendant. Where counsel failed to investigate, defendants are faulted for failing to show what that investigation would have uncovered. Where counsel failed to prepare for trial, defendants are faulted for failing to demonstrate how preparation would have altered the outcome. The absence created by counsel's failure is treated as proof that the failure did not matter. Failure generates its own insulation.

At this stage, defendants are typically proceeding pro se. Counsel has withdrawn. The record is fixed. Yet the ineffective assistance standard analysis continues to demand proof that presumes access to information the defendant does not possess. The defendant is expected to become the functional equivalent of counsel, without the credentials or capacity to do so. Courts routinely deny pro se defendants access to discovery, investigative materials, and case records, even where no safety or confidentiality concern exists. That denial is discretionary, and it is decisive. The analysis is then applied as if access had existed, even though it was explicitly denied.

Ineffective assistance of counsel thus presumes the availability of information necessary to establish prejudice while permitting courts to withhold that information by choice. Discretion. Defendants are required to prove what competent representation would have revealed while being barred from the very materials that could show it. The inability to satisfy the standard is treated as substantive weakness rather than the predictable result of procedural exclusion.

This circularity is not incidental. It is structural. The more completely counsel failed to develop the case, the less there is to point to. Serious failures produce empty records. Empty records justify denial. Denial is reinforced by discretionary refusals to allow discovery or evidentiary development. The most damaging breakdowns become the least remediable.

In this way, prejudice analysis completes the work that deference begins. If failure is alleged, it is deferred to strategy. If deficiency is conceded, it is neutralized through non-prejudicial determinations grounded in discretion designed to preserve finality. At no point is the right to counsel tested through inquiry into what competent representation would have required. It is extinguished through discretion and closure.

Timing and the Fixed Record

Ineffective assistance claims are almost never resolved at the moment failure occurs. They are structurally deferred until after conviction. By the time they are heard, the trial is over, the verdict is final, and the record is fixed.

This timing is not incidental. It is decisive. Enforcement that begins only after liberty has been taken cannot function as protection. It can only function as review, and even that review is constrained by a record that already reflects the consequences of counsel's failures rather than their cause, scope, or impact.

The system thus places Sixth Amendment enforcement at the point where it is least capable of producing correction. There is no requirement that courts examine counsel's performance while the proceeding is ongoing. There is no obligation to interrupt deficient representation, to demand justification, or to develop a record of adequacy. The opportunity for intervention is allowed to pass, and the resulting harm is later treated as an unavoidable feature of the case rather than the product of judicial inaction.

Once the record is fixed, absence becomes authoritative. Missing objections, undeveloped facts, untested theories, and unexplored defenses are preserved not as failures to be remedied, but as silences to be respected. Courts then evaluate prejudice by reference to what the record contains, even though the claim asserts that the record is incomplete precisely because of counsel's deficiency.

Timing converts enforcement into speculation. Courts are asked to reconstruct hypothetical proceedings without the tools to test them. Defendants are required to prove what would have happened in a trial that never occurred, using a record shaped by the very failures under review. The burden is shifted onto those least able to carry it, at the stage where access to evidence, counsel, and meaningful development is most restricted. The timing is never right for a review that matters to the defendant.

What emerges is not delayed enforcement, but disabled enforcement. By fixing the record before adequacy is examined, the system ensures that review occurs only after meaningful correction is no longer possible. The Sixth Amendment remains formally intact, but its operation is confined to a moment when intervention has already been rendered impossible.

Institutional Tension and Structural Resolution

Ineffective assistance claims do not arise in a neutral posture. Courts are asked to assess the adequacy of counsel that the court itself selected, appointed, or approved to represent the defendant. That selection reflects an affirmative judgment that the lawyer was competent to carry the case forward and capable of providing constitutionally adequate representation.

This posture creates an institutional tension that cannot be avoided. A finding of ineffectiveness is not only a judgment about an individual lawyer's performance. It requires acknowledging that representation previously deemed acceptable was allowed to proceed despite constitutional deficiency, and that the proceeding continued without correction. The inquiry therefore implicates both the conduct of counsel and the court's own prior judgment.

This tension is resolved by relocating enforcement rather than confronting it directly. Review is deferred until after conviction, when the proceeding has concluded and the record is fixed. Standards are framed through deference rather than examination. Omissions are presumed strategic rather than deficient. Adequacy is assessed indirectly, through speculative outcome analysis, rather than through contemporaneous evaluation of representation.

This relocation matters. By postponing review and narrowing its scope, the structure avoids requiring courts to assess whether earlier intervention was necessary or whether deficient representation should have been interrupted while the proceeding was ongoing. The question becomes whether the defendant can now satisfy a heightened burden within a closed record, rather than whether the proceeding should have been corrected when failure occurred.

What appears as neutral sequencing thus functions as insulation. Enforcement is permitted only at a stage where correction threatens finality rather than fairness. Review is not denied but it is channeled into a form that minimizes disruption to judgments that are already rendered and confidence that is already placed.

In this way, institutional tension is not eliminated. It is managed. The system absorbs the consequences of prior judgment by converting questions of adequacy into questions of prejudice and closure, ensuring that the system can acknowledge the right, while limiting the occasions on which it must confront its own decisions.

Containment Through Discretion

Discretion is the mechanism through which legal limits are enforced without being named. It operates at every stage of ineffective assistance review, shaping not only outcomes but the scope of inquiry itself. While the right to counsel is framed as mandatory, the tools necessary to enforce that right are routinely treated as discretionary.

Courts exercise discretion over whether to appoint counsel, permit discovery, expand the record, hold evidentiary hearings, or allow development beyond the trial transcript. Each of these decisions determines whether an ineffective assistance claim can be meaningfully examined. Yet none is guaranteed. The availability of enforcement depends not on the presence of alleged constitutional failure, but on whether the court elects to allow inquiry to proceed.

This discretionary posture is decisive because ineffective assistance claims almost always arise in contexts where the defendant lacks access to evidence, legal representation, or the means to develop proof independently. Many defendants raise these claims while proceeding pro se, after conviction, without counsel, discovery, or investigative support. Without judicial permission, the claim remains confined to a record created under the very deficiencies that are being challenged. Discretion thus determines whether review will be substantive or merely formal.

Containment occurs through discretion. A decision to deny discovery limits factual development. A decision to deny a hearing preserves the existing record. A decision to deny counsel leaves the defendant responsible for articulating complex legal and factual claims alone. Each choice appears narrow and case specific. Together, they ensure that enforcement rarely advances beyond threshold review.

For the indigent defendant, discretion is not a neutral gatekeeping function. It determines whether enforcement is possible at all. Review is permitted in theory, but only on terms that the defendant cannot satisfy. Access to evidence depends on permission. Legal development depends on appointment. Factual inquiry depends on judicial willingness to allow discovery or examination beyond the existing record. When discretion is exercised to deny these tools, the claim is defeated before it is examined.

This dynamic is most visible in the denial of discovery. Claims of ineffective assistance frequently depend on materials outside of the trial record, including communications, charging representations, and pretrial proceedings that shaped the case. Yet courts routinely refuse discovery, citing finality, speculation, or the absence of proof. Or, no reason at all, simply because the court said so. The defendant is then faulted for failing to substantiate allegations that could only be verified through access to the very materials that are withheld.

The contradiction is structural. The defendant is ordinarily guaranteed the right to confront the evidence presented by the state. But when ineffective assistance is raised, particularly by a pro se defendant, that guarantee quietly recedes. The claim turns not on confronting adverse testimony at trial, but on challenging counsel's failure to contest the government's case, often without counsel, discovery, or a hearing. What would be impermissible in an adversarial proceeding becomes routine in post-conviction review.

Discretion permits this inversion. Courts evaluate claims of deficient representation while denying the mechanisms through which deficiency could be tested. The defendant is required to prove failure without the ability to confront it, to establish prejudice without access to the facts that would demonstrate it, and to litigate the adequacy of counsel without counsel at all. The right to confrontation remains formally intact, but it is functionally suspended at the moment it would matter most.

This is not an accidental outcome. Discretion operates as the system's pressure valve. It allows courts to acknowledge the right to counsel while controlling the conditions under which that right may be enforced. Constitutional failure does not trigger investigation. It triggers restraint. The more consequential the allegation, the more discretion is invoked to prevent its development.

The result is a form of review that preserves legitimacy while foreclosing correction. The right remains intact, the standard is recited, and the process appears open. But discretion ensures that consideration occurs without the tools necessary to test it. What is called review functions as denial, and what is framed as restraint becomes the mechanism through which enforcement is quietly extinguished. The system often claims justification after the fact, but operates first on power.

Let's be honest: Sometimes Discretion is just authority untethered from explanation.

Why The Legal System Acknowledges Failure, Yet Never Corrects It

Taken together, the structural processes that govern ineffective assistance do not function as mechanisms of correction. They function as systems of containment. Each feature: deference, prejudice, timing, discretion, and finality, narrows the conditions under which enforcement may occur. When aligned, they ensure that constitutional failure is acknowledged only in forms that do not threaten completed judgments.

The structure also redistributes burden. The defendant must identify failure without access to evidence, demonstrate harm within a closed record, and overcome presumptions that favor prior proceedings. For indigent and pro se defendants, this burden is effectively insurmountable. Enforcement is available in name, but unattainable in practice.

What results is a system that treats failure as something to be managed rather than remedied. Claims are reviewed, standards are recited, and denials are issued. But the architecture ensures that review occurs under conditions where meaningful relief is unlikely. Correction becomes exceptional not because violations are rare, but because the system is designed to resist reopening what has already been decided.

This containment serves institutional stability. It preserves confidence in prior judgments, protects discretionary authority, and avoids confronting the human and procedural limits that shaped the proceeding. The Sixth Amendment remains formally intact, but its enforcement is displaced into a posture where acknowledgment does not require action.

In this way, the system does not eliminate the right to counsel. It neutralizes its force. The promise of representation survives, while the mechanisms necessary to enforce that promise are systematically constrained. What appears as fidelity to process becomes a method of preserving outcomes.

The result is a constitutional guarantee that exists without any reliable means of correction. Enforcement disappears not through
rejection, but through design. At this point, formal reasoning alone
is insufficient, because the persistence of these outcomes cannot
be understood without examining how judicial decision making
is experienced, managed, and constrained within the system itself.

The Abstraction of Decision Making

When ineffective assistance of counsel is discussed, decision making
is routinely abstracted away from the people who perform it. Courts
are treated as institutional actors, and outcomes are described as
the mechanical application of standards rather than the product of
judgment. In that abstraction, the human dimensions of adjudication disappear.

This framing is misleading. Judicial decisions are not generated by
institutions acting independently of the people who occupy them.
They are made through judgment exercised in real time, informed by
experience, professional familiarity, confidence in prior choices, and
assumptions about how proceedings should unfold. These features
are not distortions of the process. They are part of it.

Courts are not asked to evaluate ineffective assistance in the abstract.
They are asked to assess the adequacy of counsel that the court
itself selected, appointed, or approved to represent the defendant.
That selection reflects an affirmative judgment that the lawyer was
competent to carry the case forward. It is a decision grounded in

trust, reliance, and the expectation that the representation would meet constitutional standards.

This dynamic produces a conflict that courts manage rather than confront. A determination of ineffective representation does more than assess counsel's conduct. It requires acknowledging that a proceeding overseen by the court unfolded under constitutionally deficient conditions, and that the failure was permitted to continue without intervention. That recognition is not purely institutional. It is personal. It implicates the judgment, restraint, and choices of the individuals who allowed the proceeding to move forward. Abstraction becomes the mechanism through which that discomfort is avoided. By shifting the inquiry from lived representation to an abstract formulation, the system distances decision makers from the human consequences of their own oversight. Error may be acknowledged in theory, but responsibility is diffused through language that conceals the human role in allowing the failure to persist.

The same abstraction erases the human consequences for counsel. A judicial finding that representation was constitutionally ineffective is not a neutral legal conclusion. It carries reputational weight. It can affect careers, professional standing, future appointments, and credibility within the legal community. Courts are not blind to this reality. Yet the systems structure treats the designation of ineffectiveness as though it were a purely technical assessment, detached from its real-world impact on both the lawyer involved and the court's own prior judgment.

Adjudication does not occur in a vacuum. Judges and lawyers operate within overlapping professional networks. Many judges were themselves prosecutors or defense attorneys in the same offices that now appear before them. The difficulty of sanctioning a prosecutor with whom one once worked, or declaring ineffective a lawyer long regarded as competent, is not a moral failing. It is an ordinary feature of human judgment operating within institutional roles.

The systems design accommodates this reality by removing it from view. Review is deferred. Standards are narrowed. Deference replaces examination. By speaking in institutional terms, the law presents outcomes as inevitable consequences of structure rather than discretionary choices shaped by confidence, reliance, and the human costs of condemnation. Deference appears neutral. Timing appears procedural. Finality appears necessary.

Discretion controls it all.

What is often left unspoken is that the recognition of judgment itself can be experienced as destabilizing within adjudication. When ineffective assistance or misconduct is clear, acknowledging the role of judgment does not merely identify error. It threatens the premise that the robe transforms decision making into something categorically different. In that posture, to name the human element can feel less like description and more like accusation.

This reaction is not necessarily conscious. It does not require defensiveness or bad faith. It arises from the structure of the role itself. Judicial authority depends on the perception that decisions flow from law rather than from the ordinary limits, loyalties, and constraints that shape all judgment. When a ruling implicitly acknowledges that those forces were present and operative, the authority of the decision can feel diminished rather than clarified.

The process responds by reasserting abstraction. Misconduct becomes error review. Ineffectiveness becomes deference. Judgment becomes process. By recasting decision making as institutional output, the law avoids the discomfort of acknowledging that adjudication is carried out by people operating within networks of trust, reputation, experience, and restraint. What might otherwise be understood as a natural limitation of judgment is treated as an affront to the role itself.

The cost of this abstraction is not merely analytical. It reshapes enforcement. When acknowledging judgment is perceived as undermining authority, correction becomes rare and condemnation becomes exceptional. The system protects itself by insisting that judgment was never human in the first place. What remains is a legal structure that speaks in neutral terms while quietly insulating the people who must apply it.

This is not a failure of character. It is a failure of candor. A system that cannot acknowledge the human dimensions of its own decision making cannot correct them. In that silence, enforcement does not disappear through rejection, but through refusal to name what is plainly present.

Simply: The system functions by refusing to acknowledge the humanity that is plainly operating within its decisions.

Finality as the Unwritten Rule

Finality operates as the governing principle of Sixth Amendment enforcement, even though it is rarely named as such. Once judgment is entered, preservation of that judgment becomes the overriding priority. Review is organized not around accuracy, not around correction, and not around the enforcement of constitutional rights, but around protecting the stability of the outcome already reached. Finality is being chosen over constitutional enforcement.

This prioritization reshapes the posture of ineffective assistance review from the outset. Claims are not examined as opportunities to enforce the Sixth Amendment's guarantee of effective assistance of counsel. They are treated as challenges to settled results. The central question is no longer whether representation was constitutionally adequate, but whether enforcing the Constitution would disturb finality. In this posture, enforcement is no longer the objective. Finality is.

There can be no legitimate finality in a constitutionally deficient proceeding. Finality presumes that the process leading to judgment was fair, reliable, and consistent with constitutional guarantees. When those guarantees were not enforced, finality does not represent closure. It represents the preservation of an uncorrected constitutional violation. Yet post-conviction review proceeds as though the conclusion of the case itself cures any defect.

Once judgment is entered, finality is treated as an independent value, capable of outweighing accuracy, correction, and constitutional enforcement. A conviction is deemed complete not because it was constitutionally sound, but because it has concluded. In that inversion, constitutional deficiency becomes tolerable so long as it is stable. The Constitution yields not to law, but to closure.

Finality is prioritized over accuracy. Courts do not ask whether deficient representation produced an unreliable verdict. They ask whether reopening the case would undermine stability. The burden shifts away from the government's obligation to ensure a fair proceeding and onto the defendant's obligation to justify disrupting a completed one. Constitutional error is absorbed so long as it does not threaten the durability of the judgment.

Finality is prioritized over correction. Because ineffective assistance is examined only after proceedings conclude, courts rely on a record created without contemporaneous scrutiny of counsel's performance. Deficiencies that should have prompted intervention are preserved as settled facts. Omissions are no longer treated as failures to be remedied, but as features of a finished case. What could have been corrected becomes untouchable.

In this structure, finality transforms absence into permanence. The absence of objections is treated as waiver. The absence of evidence is treated as confirmation that none existed. The absence of inquiry is treated as a reason to deny it. The very gaps produced by ineffective representation are converted into proof that no constitutional violation occurred. What is missing becomes dispositive precisely because inquiry is foreclosed.

Finality is also prioritized over enforcement of constitutional rights themselves. Once judgment is entered, rights are presumed satisfied.

Violations are acknowledged only insofar as they do not require action. The Sixth Amendment survives as language, but its enforcement is subordinated to outcome preservation. Courts do not deny the right. They deny its operation.

Layered review reinforces this choice. Appellate courts defer to trial courts. Post-conviction courts defer to both. Each level invokes restraint, procedural posture, and respect for prior proceedings. What appears as multiple opportunities for review functions instead as a closed loop in which finality gains strength at every stage and constitutional enforcement becomes increasingly remote.

In this way, finality does not merely limit relief. It reorders constitutional priorities. Accuracy yields to closure. Correction yields to stability. Enforcement yields to preservation. Finality is not a neutral background value. It is the rule that determines when constitutional violations will be tolerated rather than remedied.

The result is a constitutional guarantee that remains formally intact but practically constrained. Review proceeds, standards are recited, and denials are issued, while the underlying violations remain untouched. The system does not reject the Sixth Amendment. It preserves outcomes at its expense.

Each of these mechanisms are presented as a safeguard. Harmless error review, ineffective assistance standards, prejudice analysis, procedural default, and deference to counsel's purported strategy are all described as mechanisms designed to protect the defendant and preserve the integrity of adjudication. In practice, they function otherwise. Each operates as a filter that shifts the inquiry away from the jury and toward the judge. Each allows acknowledged constitutional failure to be absorbed rather than corrected. And each leads to the same endpoint: judicial substitution for the jury under the guise of appellate review. What are framed as protections do not restrain error. They normalize it.

The system treats finality as inevitable, but it never answers the prior question: who decided that the end of litigation should matter more than the correctness of the result. Finality is enforced as though it were synonymous with justice, even when it plainly functions to foreclose it.

Across these accepted practices, the pattern does not vary. The consequences of this structure are not abstract. It is clear, and it is:

The statutory meaning of rights no longer governs. Discretion does.

What This Chapter Establishes

This chapter establishes that the disappearance of Sixth Amendment enforcement did not occur at the level of principle. It occurred at the level of remedy. The right to counsel remains formally intact, but the mechanisms necessary to enforce that right have been systematically constrained.

Ineffective assistance laws preserve the constitutional guarantee in theory while channeling its enforcement into postures where correction is unlikely. By deferring review, constraining inquiry, elevating discretion, and prioritizing finality, the system ensures that constitutional failure can be acknowledged without requiring meaningful action. Enforcement is not rejected. It is displaced.

This architecture explains why constitutional deficiency can be visible yet unremedied. Deference shields prior judgments. Prejudice reframes violation as speculation. Timing fixes the record before adequacy is examined. Discretion governs access to the tools of inquiry, and prejudice, and deference. Finality is chosen over constitutional enforcement. Each feature appears defensible in isolation. Together, they foreclose correction.

The chapters that follow trace how this containment model extends beyond formal legal standards into appellate review, post-conviction proceedings, and administrative oversight. What appears as layered protection operates instead as a closed loop, reinforcing non enforcement at every stage. The right to counsel remains intact in language, while its enforcement quietly recedes from view.

Chapter 3
Appellate Review and the Illusion of Correction

The Promise of Appellate Correction

Appellate review is often described as the institutional safeguard that corrects trial level error. It is portrayed as the forum where constitutional violations are finally taken seriously, where distance from trial allows objectivity, and where failures in representation or procedure are identified and remedied. That description carries enormous legitimacy. It reassures courts, lawyers, and the public that error will not be allowed to stand.

This posture governs how ineffective assistance claims are received. They are not approached as opportunities for correction, but as challenges to results that have already acquired institutional weight. The inquiry is calibrated to protect the judgment, not to test the representation that produced it. The question is no longer whether counsel's performance met constitutional standards, but whether any deficiency is so obvious, so fully documented, and so consequential that preservation becomes untenable.

Uncertainty therefore does not invite inquiry. It resolves in favor of affirmance.

This assumption reshapes how finality enters appellate analysis. Finality is not argued for or justified. It is presumed. Appellate orders speak of the judgment as settled, complete, and entitled to stability as a matter of course. Constitutional claims are therefore reviewed not against the baseline of enforcement, but against the background expectation that the judgment should stand.

Finality as Presumption on Appeal

On appeal, finality is not treated as a value to be weighed. It is treated as a condition that already exists. Appellate courts do not ask whether finality should prevail over constitutional enforcement. They proceed as though that question has already been answered.

This presumption shapes appellate review before any claim is considered. The judgment arrives cloaked in legitimacy simply by virtue of having been entered, entitled to stability but not required to demonstrate constitutional correctness. The conviction is treated as settled, the proceeding as complete, and the outcome as entitled to preservation. Constitutional claims therefore enter appellate review not as assertions of unremedied violation, but as disruptions to an order that is presumed sound.

Finality is not justified on appeal. It is normalized. Appellate orders routinely speak of closure, restraint, and the limited role of review as ordinary features of appellate responsibility. The preservation of the judgment is treated as common sense rather than choice. The burden is placed entirely on the defendant to explain why finality should yield, even when the claim asserts that constitutional guarantees were never enforced in the first place.

Finality does not answer whether the Sixth Amendment was honored. It answers whether the system will continue to ask. Once finality governs, Sixth Amendment enforcement is no longer a question of right, but of whether inquiry is permitted to persist at all.

The presumption of finality also governs the tone and structure of appellate review. Claims are framed narrowly. Standards are invoked early. Deference is emphasized before inquiry begins. The possibility of constitutional error is acknowledged abstractly, while the risk of disruption to the judgment is treated as concrete and immediate. In this balance, stability consistently outweighs enforcement.

This is how appellate review comes to protect judgments rather than test them. Finality does not merely influence outcomes. It governs the posture of review itself. Before the merits are reached, the conclusion is already favored.

What appears as restraint is therefore a choice. Finality is being chosen over constitutional enforcement. The appeal proceeds, the opinion is written, and the judgment stands, not because the constitutional claim lacked force, but because finality was presumed to matter more.

Standards of Review as Outcome Protection

Standards of review are presented as neutral rules governing appellate restraint. They are framed as technical devices that allocate authority between trial and appellate courts. In the context of Sixth Amendment enforcement, they function as mechanisms of outcome protection.

Ineffective assistance claims on appeal are evaluated under layers of deference that sharply constrain judicial intervention. Findings of fact are reviewed for clear error. Strategic judgments are presumed reasonable. Mixed questions are framed in ways that favor affirmance. Each standard narrows the range of permissible correction and shifts the burden onto defendants to demonstrate error with a level of precision that the record rarely permits.

This deference is not incidental. It is structural. Standards of review determine not only how much weight appellate courts give to trial level decisions, but how willing they are to revisit them at all. By the time a case reaches appeal, the combination of deferential review and a fixed record ensures that most claims of deficient representation are filtered out before meaningful engagement occurs.

The effect is cumulative and self-reinforcing. Where the record is thin, courts defer to trial level determinations. Where omissions appear, they are attributed to strategy. Where uncertainty exists, it is resolved in favor of the judgment. Each layer of review operates as a narrowing gate, reducing constitutional inquiry until enforcement becomes functionally unavailable.

Even when appellate courts acknowledge potential concerns, standards of review often supply the reason relief cannot be granted. Error may be identified but deemed insufficiently clear. Deficiency may be assumed but treated as immaterial. The posture of review allows courts to recognize problems without acting on them.

In this way, standards of review preserve judgments while maintaining the appearance of constitutional oversight. The Sixth Amendment is not ignored. It is evaluated through a lens calibrated to favor stability over correction. Review proceeds, legal standards are applied, and outcomes remain intact.

What is protected is not the constitutional right itself, but the judgment entered beneath it. When judgments are treated as needing protection, factual impossibility does not operate as a stopping point. It becomes a problem of framing rather than proof. Courts ask whether a theory can sustain a verdict, not whether the record actually establishes the conduct alleged. Once that shift occurs, contradictions are absorbed rather than confronted.

Ineffective Assistance on Direct Appeal

Although ineffective assistance claims may technically be raised on direct appeal, appellate courts rarely adjudicate them there. Courts do not simply state that the record is inadequate. They emphasize that appellate review is limited to the existing record, that credibility determinations and factual development are unavailable, and that ineffective assistance claims are therefore better suited to collateral proceedings where evidence can be developed. The refrain is familiar: direct appeal is not the proper forum, post-conviction review is.

This deferral is framed as protective, even benevolent. Courts explain that postponement preserves the defendant's ability to fully litigate the claim later. In the meantime, however, the defendant remains bound by a final judgment. The conviction is affirmed. The sentence is executed. Liberty is lost. Whatever deficiencies in representation may have occurred are acknowledged abstractly but left unexamined while the consequences of those deficiencies are fully imposed.

By declining to adjudicate ineffective assistance on direct appeal, appellate courts allow deficient representation to escape contemporaneous scrutiny at the only moment when correction could still matter. The record remains fixed. The appeal concludes. Finality begins to attach. The opportunity for intervention passes, not because the claim lacked substance, but because the posture of review made engagement inconvenient.

When the claim later reappears in post-conviction proceedings, it does so under a different and far more restrictive regime. The defendant now bears a heightened burden. Access to evidence is limited. Discovery is discretionary. The same record appellate courts deemed insufficient for review is now treated as definitive. What could not be evaluated earlier becomes impossible to reconstruct later, and uncertainty is resolved in favor of the judgment.

This is where finality quietly enters the analysis. Courts become reluctant to disturb a judgment that has already been affirmed, executed, and relied upon. The passage of time is treated as neutral, even though delay was structurally imposed by the system itself. The longer the claim has gone unadjudicated, the heavier the institutional weight of the judgment becomes.

The result is a procedural loop. Appellate courts decline review because the record is undeveloped. Post-conviction courts deny relief because the record is closed. Each stage defers responsibility to the next, while finality hardens in the background. Enforcement is postponed until it is no longer viable.

This cycle does not merely delay Sixth Amendment enforcement. It disables it. By routing ineffective assistance claims away from direct appeal and into a forum where correction is structurally constrained and finality already entrenched, the system ensures that acknowledgment replaces action. The right is preserved in theory, while enforcement recedes precisely at the moments when it would require disruption of an affirmed judgment.

Appellate Counsel and Compounded Absence

Appellate enforcement of the Sixth Amendment depends not only on formal legal standards, but on the quality of appellate representation. Yet failures at this stage are frequently invisible, unreviewed, and insulated from consequence.

Appellate counsel controls the aperture of review. Decisions about which issues to raise, which omissions to challenge, and how claims are framed determine what the appellate court is permitted to consider. When appellate counsel declines to raise ineffective assistance, fails to confront trial level omissions, or narrows issues to avoid disruption, those choices define the boundaries of appellate review itself. What is not raised does not exist for purposes of enforcement.

In many cases, particularly where counsel is court appointed, trial and appellate counsel are the same attorney. In those circumstances, appellate silence does not merely reflect strategic choice. It functions as self-insulation. Failures at trial are unlikely to be challenged on appeal by the same counsel who committed them. The absence of challenge is then attributed to professional judgment rather than structural conflict.

Failures at the appellate stage do not merely mirror earlier deficiencies. They compound them. Trial level omissions become fixed in the record. Appellate silence transforms those omissions into settled features of the case. Each unchallenged absence hardens into a baseline that subsequent review is stuck with, rather than a deficiency to be examined.

Review of appellate counsel's effectiveness is even more constrained than review of trial counsel. Courts presume competence, defer to strategic judgment, and require proof of prejudice within an already restricted record. The defendant must demonstrate not only that appellate counsel erred, but that raising additional claims would have altered the outcome of an appeal already shaped by silence. In this posture, absence once again becomes proof.

This structure permits ineffective assistance to occur at multiple levels without triggering enforcement. Each stage relies on the assumed integrity of the prior one. Each failure is shielded by deference to the next. What began as a lapse in representation becomes a cumulative barrier to correction.

The result is not a single constitutional violation, but a layered disappearance of constitutional rights. By the time ineffective assistance reaches the point of review, it has passed through too many presumptions, too many deferrals, and too many fixed records to be meaningfully addressed. Enforcement remains theoretically available, but practically unreachable.

The Fixed Record on Appeal

Appellate review proceeds on a fixed record. That constraint is often described as a neutral feature of appellate practice, a necessary boundary that preserves orderly review. In the context of Sixth Amendment enforcement, it is decisive.

By the time a case reaches appeal, the record has already been shaped by the quality of representation under review. Decisions not to object, investigate, cross examine, or develop evidence are preserved not as failures, but as absences. Appellate courts then assess constitutional adequacy by reference to what the record contains, even though the claim itself asserts that the record is incomplete precisely because counsel failed to perform.

This posture converts trial level failure into appellate limitation. The appellate court does not ask what the proceeding would have looked like had representation been effective. It asks whether the existing record demonstrates error clearly enough to justify reversal.

Where counsel's failures left no trace, appellate review treats silence as confirmation rather than absence.

The fixed record also interacts with deference in a way that fore-closes inquiry. Appellate courts presume that trial proceedings were conducted properly and that counsel's choices were reasonable. Without a developed record to the contrary, omissions are attributed to strategy and gaps are treated as immaterial. The absence of evidence becomes a reason to affirm rather than a signal that inquiry was required.

This structure places defendants in a paradoxical position. They must demonstrate constitutional inadequacy using a record that reflects the very failures that they challenge. Where counsel failed to preserve objections or develop facts, appellate courts lack both the tools and the institutional posture to reconstruct what was lost. Review proceeds, but correction remains elusive.

In this way, the fixed record on appeal does not merely limit what appellate courts can see. It determines what they are willing to question. The right to effective assistance is acknowledged, but its enforcement is confined to what survived representation that may itself have been constitutionally deficient.

The Fixed Record as Outcome Protection

The fixed record is often justified as a limitation inherent in appellate courts' institutional role. In practice, it functions as a mechanism of outcome protection. It confines review to boundaries that favor preservation over correction and ensures that appellate scrutiny occurs only within a record already shaped by the representation under challenge.

Where counsel failed to develop evidence, appellate courts presume that none existed. Where counsel failed to object, appellate courts presume waiver. Where counsel failed to investigate, appellate courts presume irrelevance. Each presumption resolves uncertainty in favor of finality rather than inquiry. Absence is converted into acceptance, and silence is treated as confirmation.

This structure does not merely restrict appellate authority. It directs it. Appellate courts are positioned to review outcomes, not to reconstruct what effective representation might have produced. Because the record has already absorbed the effects of deficient performance, review begins from a posture that assumes completeness. The question shifts from whether the Sixth Amendment was violated to whether the violation can be demonstrated without unsettling an already stabilized judgment.

Once framed this way, enforcement becomes conditional on preservation. Violations that leave no trace in the record are functionally immune from correction. The very deficiencies that undermine constitutional adequacy become the reason relief is unavailable. The record is treated as neutral, even though it is the product of the failures being reviewed.

In this way, the fixed record operates as a structural firewall. It allows appellate courts to perform review while preventing meaningful intervention. The right to counsel remains formally intact, but its enforcement is confined to what survives representation that may itself have been constitutionally deficient. What is protected is not the integrity of the proceeding, but the judgment that emerged from it.

The Illusion of Correction

Taken together, appellate review does not correct the failures that occurred below. It legitimizes them. Claims are reviewed, opinions are issued, and judgments are affirmed. The process appears thorough, even when enforcement never meaningfully occurs.

This illusion is sustained by structure, not by neglect. Deference limits inquiry. Standards of review protect outcomes. The fixed record constrains what can be seen. Deferral displaces enforcement. At every stage, appellate review reinforces the architecture described in Chapter Two. Each mechanism narrows the space for correction while preserving the appearance of constitutional engagement.

The appearance of correction matters. It allows the system to claim fidelity to constitutional guarantees while avoiding disruption of completed judgments. The Sixth Amendment is invoked, analyzed, and applied. Yet enforcement is filtered through institutional practices calibrated to preserve stability rather than to remedy constitutional failure.

The fixed record plays a decisive role in sustaining this illusion. It converts the consequences of deficient representation into permanent features of the case. Omissions are treated as choices. Silence is treated as sufficiency. What is missing is not interrogated, but absorbed. Review proceeds as though the record were neutral, even though it reflects the very failures under examination.

At this stage appellate review functions less as a safeguard than as a seal. It confers legitimacy on outcomes already reached and closes the window for meaningful intervention. Correction is theoretically available, but structurally inaccessible. The system moves forward, not because constitutional adequacy has been confirmed, but because procedure has been completed.

What remains is a right that survives in language but not in operation. The Sixth Amendment endures as a formal guarantee, invoked at every stage of review. Yet its enforcement recedes behind layers of institutional reasoning designed to preserve judgments rather than to confront the conditions under which they were produced.

This is not the absence of review. It is the substitution of review for enforcement.

What This Chapter Establishes

This chapter establishes that appellate review does not merely inherit the consequences of ineffective representation. It institutionalizes them.

By fixing the record before constitutional adequacy is meaningfully examined, appellate review converts silence, omission, and absence into structural barriers to enforcement. What is missing is not treated as a signal for inquiry, but as a limit on review. The Sixth Amendment is acknowledged, but its protection is measured only against what survives representation that may itself have been constitutionally deficient.

Appellate review thus operates within a closed evidentiary and analytical frame. Deference, standards of review, and record constraints work together to preserve judgments rather than to interrogate the conditions under which they were produced. What cannot be proven within the inherited record is treated as immaterial, even when the absence of proof is the very harm that is alleged.

The chapters that follow trace how this containment model extends beyond the record itself. The same logic reappears in appellate posture, jurisdictional deflection, and the prioritization of finality. What is presented as layered protection functions instead as a closed loop. Review occurs. Opinions issue. Judgments endure. But constitutional enforcement is displaced at every stage where it would require disruption.

The result is not the denial of the right to counsel, but its systematic neutralization. The Sixth Amendment remains intact in structure and language, while the mechanisms capable of enforcing it quietly recede from view.

Chapter 4
The Economics of Indigent Defense and the Manufacture of Pleas

Rights Filtered Through Economics

The Sixth Amendment promises two things that are supposed to matter equally: the right to counsel and the right to trial. In the federal system, those promises exist in text and formal articulation. In practice, they are filtered through an economic structure that quietly determines how defense advocacy actually functions long before any formal review is invoked, or any appellate court ever reviews a record.

For indigent defendants, constitutional rights do not operate in a neutral legal vacuum. They operate inside of funding systems, workload realities, and institutional incentives that reward speed, discourage resistance, and move cases toward resolution and finality, often times without adjudication of the merits of the claim. What appears as a legal choice on paper is often economic coercion in operation. Decisions labeled "strategy" are frequently triage. Outcomes described as voluntary are routinely engineered.

This chapter examines how Sixth Amendment enforcement is distorted at its earliest point of contact: appointment. The disappearance of enforcement does not begin with appellate deference or finality principles. It begins when counsel is appointed without capacity, without time, and without structural support to function as an adversarial safeguard. From that moment forward, the system proceeds as though representation has been secured, even when the conditions necessary for meaningful defense have already been foreclosed.

What follows is not an argument about individual counsel or isolated failures. It is an examination of how economic design shapes constitutional outcomes. When defense systems are funded to resolve cases rather than contest them, when resistance is punished and compliance is rewarded, and when speed substitutes for scrutiny, pleas are not merely encouraged. They are manufactured.

High plea rates are later cited as proof that the system works. In reality, they are evidence that the right to trial has been made structurally irrational for those without resources. The Sixth Amendment survives in form, while its exercise is quietly priced out of reach.

Appointment Without Capacity

Indigent defense is structured around the appointment of counsel as the mechanism by which the Sixth Amendment right to counsel is deemed satisfied for defendants without resources. In practice, appointment alone does not guarantee meaningful representation.

The system does not ensure that appointed counsel has the experience, training, or subject matter knowledge necessary to defend the charges at issue. Counsel may be appointed promptly and still be structurally unprepared to defend the case that they have been assigned.

Indigent defendants are routinely charged under statutes and sentencing schemes that demand specialized knowledge, including complex fraud provisions, conspiracy laws, guideline enhancements, and regulatory frameworks. Appointment systems rarely match counsel experience to charge complexity. They prioritize availability over fit. As a result, defendants may be represented by counsel who have never litigated the governing statute, challenged the relevant evidentiary rules, or navigated the sentencing exposure that the case presents. From the outset, the adversarial process is weakened not by neglect, but by misalignment.

Timing then compounds the deficiency. Counsel may be appointed after critical early stages of the case have already shaped leverage and posture. Charging decisions, initial detention determinations, and the government's control over the flow and timing of discovery frequently occur before defense counsel has had a meaningful opportunity to investigate, contest, or influence them. Even when counsel is present early, resource constraints often limit what intervention is realistically possible.

These early stages are not procedural formalities. They are the stages at which risk is set, narratives harden, and pressure accumulates. When defense counsel lacks subject matter competence at the outset, or lacks the ability to act effectively when those decisions are made, the adversarial process does not merely weaken. It fails to take hold.

Appointment in this context functions as formal compliance rather than functional protection. The Sixth Amendment is treated as satisfied once a name is entered on the docket, regardless of whether counsel has the knowledge, time, or institutional support necessary to operate as an adversarial safeguard. The right exists on paper while its exercise is constrained in practice.

Even where appointment is timely, capacity is often absent. Excessive caseloads and inadequate funding force counsel into triage. Triage in this context does not mean prioritizing the most important work. It means rationing attention, investigation, and motion practice because there is not enough time or money to perform all of the tasks that competent representation requires. Counsel must decide which constitutional functions can be attempted and which will go undone, not as a matter of strategy, but as a matter of survival within the system.

The system nonetheless proceeds as though meaningful representation has been secured. Courts presume adequacy. Prosecutors proceed with confidence. Deadlines continue to run. The absence of informed adversarial testing is not treated as a constitutional defect requiring correction. It is treated as an operational necessity.

This is how Sixth Amendment enforcement begins to disappear before any legal analysis is invoked and before any appellate standard is applied. When counsel is appointed without the resources necessary to operate constitutionally, the adversarial process is compromised at the outset. What follows is not accidental failure, but structural non-enforcement built into the system itself.

Inquiry Treated as Hostility

Concerns about counsel competence do not arise only at the moment of appointment. They also emerge when defendants who understand their own cases observe that counsel is not operating in a genuinely adversarial role. Defendants recognize when counsel appears unfamiliar with the governing law, confused about the theory of the case, unprepared to respond to government arguments, or unable to articulate a coherent defense strategy.

When defendants raise these concerns, they are rarely treated as legitimate warnings that adversarial function may be absent. Instead, the inquiry itself is treated as a breach of order. Questions about experience or strategy are not engaged on their merits. They are framed as challenges to authority that should not have been made.

In response, counsel do not merely invoke credentials. They demand that credentials be accepted as dispositive. Years in practice or possession of a law degree are treated as conclusive proof of competence, and questioning that proof is treated as improper. Courts reinforce this posture. The distinction between formal qualification and functional performance is not examined. It is foreclosed.

At that point, the inquiry becomes a test of deference. Defendants who ask whether counsel is prepared to defend their case are characterized as hostile. Requests for explanation are treated as insubordination. Defendants are told that they do not get to decide what strategy is pursued, what motions are filed, or how the case is litigated. Assertions of exclusive control are used to end inquiry, not to justify choices. The focus shifts from whether adversarial function exists to whether the defendant has violated an expectation of submission.

Judicial responses reflect this shift. Rather than examining counsel's performance on the record, courts may redirect concerns into private meetings with counsel alone. In one documented instance, prior to a Marsden hearing addressing the adequacy of representation, the court met privately with defense counsel outside of the presence of the defendant. Such a meeting involves the court and one party without the participation of the other and removes the defendant from a discussion directly bearing on the effectiveness of their representation. The very definition of an ex parte meeting. Behind closed doors, counsel was reassured that scrutiny of performance was inappropriate and that exposure of those deficiencies was unwarranted. The focus was not on whether counsel had failed, but on containing the manner in which those failures were raised.

When this conduct was later raised through a formal complaint to the supervising judicial authority, the response did not dispute that the private meeting occurred. Instead, it redefined what the term ex parte was understood to mean. A meeting between the court and defense counsel outside of the presence of the defendant was no longer treated as an ex parte communication at all. By narrowing the definition, the inquiry was diverted away from the defendant's exclusion and toward a semantic distinction that insulated the conduct from consequence. The issue was resolved not by addressing the effect of the communication, but by revising the meaning of the rule said to govern it. Ex parte did not fail to apply. It was rewritten so that it no longer applied. Discretion working as designed.

The result was procedural containment rather than correction. In this instance, even where extensive contemporaneous documentation of ineffective assistance existed, counsel was removed not for deficient performance, but for a purported breakdown in communication. Evidence bearing directly on performance was sidelined once the issue was reframed as relational rather than constitutional. The defendant is then instructed to cooperate with replacement counsel, as though the breakdown were attributable to the defendant's conduct rather than to the documented deficiencies in representation. This directive issues even where the record reflects hostility, neglect, or constitutional failure by counsel, and even where the defendant has presented contemporaneous evidence supporting those claims. The burden is quietly reversed. The defendant is recast as the source of disruption, while the underlying ineffectiveness is treated as resolved through substitution alone. The proceeding moves forward not because the failure has been corrected, but because it has been reclassified.

In the same scenario, the court explicitly acknowledged this posture on the record. The court noted that it regularly receives complaints alleging ineffective assistance, that such complaints are ordinarily denied, and that relief is rarely granted. It then distinguished the present case not by revisiting the governing standard, but by observing that the documentation was unusually detailed. The statement is revealing. It confirms that denial is the norm, not because claims lack merit, but because they are processed through a default orientation toward rejection. Relief becomes exceptional not when constitutional standards demand it, but when a defendant's presentation exceeds the level of detail typically offered, despite the absence of discovery, investigative access, or adversarial parity.

The acknowledgment does not reflect individualized adjudication. It reflects institutional habit. The court does not ask whether ineffective assistance occurred. It asks whether the complaint has crossed an informal threshold sufficient to justify departing from a practice of routine denial. Constitutional enforcement thus turns not on violation, but on persistence, documentation, and the court's tolerance for deviation from its customary response.

This dynamic has consequences. When counsel lacks experience in a specialized area, operates without a coherent strategy, or fails to recognize critical issues, those deficiencies shape the record in irreversible ways. Experts may not be retained. Records may not be developed. Mitigation strategies may never be pursued. Technical errors are carried forward as fixed facts. Later proceedings treat those outcomes as products of professional judgment rather than as evidence of deficient performance requiring examination.

What is lost in this exchange is not civility. It is enforcement. By demanding deference to credentials, asserting unilateral control over decision making, and invoking judicial authority to suppress scrutiny, the system satisfies the Sixth Amendment through hierarchy rather than adversarial function.

Why Appointment Model Does Not Resolve Capacity or Competence

The recurring response to failures in indigent defense is procedural reassurance. If counsel is appointed, the right to counsel is treated as satisfied. If different counsel is appointed, the problem is presumed cured. This logic assumes that the mode of appointment determines the quality of representation. It does not.

The appointment model addresses presence, not capacity. It ensures that someone stands beside the defendant, not that the person has the knowledge, time, or institutional support necessary to function as an adversarial check on the government. Whether counsel is drawn from a federal defender office or appointed under a panel system, the constitutional question remains the same: can this counsel perform the functions the Sixth Amendment presupposes.

Capacity is shaped by workload, resources, timing, and specialization. Appointment does not alter those conditions. A defender with an unmanageable caseload does not gain capacity by virtue of institutional affiliation. A panel attorney unfamiliar with a complex statutory scheme does not gain competence through formal designation. The structure remains unchanged, and the same constraints operate regardless of who is assigned.

Competence is likewise not guaranteed by appointment. Legal licensure establishes minimum qualification, not case-specific preparedness. Experience in one category of cases does not translate automatically to another. Yet appointment systems rarely assess fit between counsel and charge complexity. They assume interchangeability. The result is representation that may be formally valid but functionally misaligned with the demands of the case.

This does not mean that appointed counsel lacks competence in all respects. Many are skilled advocates within particular domains. The failure arises when appointment systems treat competence as interchangeable, assigning counsel to matters that demand expertise they have not been given the capacity or opportunity to develop.

When deficiencies become visible, the system responds by substitution rather than examination. Counsel is replaced, not evaluated. The question asked is whether the attorney client relationship can be restored, not whether the representation provided met constitutional requirements. The appointment model allows substitution to operate as a reset, wiping away unresolved failures without addressing their cause.

This dynamic is especially pronounced where courts treat dissatisfaction as a communication problem rather than a signal of incapacity or incompetence. Once the issue is reframed in that way, the remedy is reassignment, not inquiry. The same structural conditions persist. The same pressures remain. The appearance of correction substitutes for enforcement.

The Sixth Amendment does not promise a rotating presence of counsel. It presupposes adversarial function. That function requires more than appointment. It requires capacity to investigate, competence to challenge, and institutional conditions that permit resistance rather than compliance. An appointment model that ignores those prerequisites does not enforce the right to counsel. It manages its appearance.

Funding as Structural Constraint

Public defense systems operate under chronic underfunding. Caseloads routinely exceed ethical recommendations. Investigative budgets are limited, delayed, or nonexistent. Expert funding is discretionary and often discouraged. Motion practice, while free to file, requires time, investigation, and supporting resources that the system routinely withholds.

These conditions do not merely burden counsel. They shape advocacy itself. Strategic decisions are made within an environment where time, money, and institutional tolerance are scarce. Choices that appear tactical from the outside are often economic from the inside.

When resources are constrained, advocacy is triaged. Counsel must decide which issues can be pursued and which must be abandoned, not based on legal merit, but on feasibility. Investigation becomes selective. Motions become exceptional rather than routine. Experts are reserved for rare cases deemed worth the expenditure of limited resources. The defense function narrows, not because claims lack merit, but because the system does not provide the resources necessary to support their development.

This constraint operates long before trial. Limited funding affects whether counsel can independently verify the government's evidence, test forensic claims, or develop alternative narratives. Without investigative capacity, discovery is simply received rather than interrogated, resulting in practical acquiescence to the government's case.

Courts are not blind to these realities, but they are structured to absorb them. Requests for funding are scrutinized more aggressively than prosecutorial expenditures. Delays are attributed to defense inefficiency rather than systemic scarcity. The denial of resources is treated as administrative discretion, not as a constitutional impairment. The record reflects compliance, even as adversarial testing recedes.

Over time, these economic constraints normalize a diminished form of defense advocacy. What should be baseline functions become extraordinary requests. What should be expected resistance is reframed as obstruction. The system adjusts its expectations downward, and constitutional adequacy is recalibrated to match what the funding structure allows rather than what the Sixth Amendment requires.

Funding, in this context, is not a background condition. It is a governing force. It determines the scope of inquiry, the depth of the challenge, and the boundaries of resistance. An indigent defense system that is structurally underfunded does not merely struggle to protect constitutional rights. It redefines them to fit the budget.

Volume Over Validity

When courts are confronted with multi-count indictments, adjudication quietly changes character. What should be a series of discrete legal inquiries, each charge tested independently against its statutory elements, becomes a holistic assessment of the case's overall weight.

Once that shift occurs, volume begins to substitute for validity. The question is no longer whether each count stands on its own as a matter of law, but whether the case, taken as a whole, appears substantial enough to justify conviction. In that environment, weak charges are not eliminated. They are absorbed.

This transformation does not occur because the law authorizes it. It occurs because discretion enters where enforcement should have been mandatory. Courts possess the authority to demand elemental proof for every count, to sever charges that lack independence, and to dismiss accusations unsupported by the record. But instead of exercising that authority to enforce statutory boundaries, courts often use discretion to relax them. Discretion becomes the means by which volume is tolerated. What should function as judgment becomes accommodation.

Each count should represent a separate accusation governed by its own statute, elements, and burden of proof. A defendant is not charged with a case. A defendant is charged with crimes. Yet in practice, once an indictment reaches a certain size, courts begin to treat it as a single narrative object. The elements remain intact in theory while enforcement recedes in practice. Courts assure themselves that deficiencies can be sorted later, that juries can compartmentalize, and that any remaining errors are harmless in light of the case as a whole. Validity is no longer enforced at the threshold. It is deferred.

This is how volume overtakes validity. Not through the absence of law, but through the discretionary suspension of its application. The accumulation of charges creates an appearance of inevitability, and discretion is used to preserve that appearance rather than interrogate it. What enters the courtroom as a set of statutory claims exits as a consolidated judgment shaped by weight and scale. Validity becomes secondary. Discretion governs.

The Trial Penalty and Charge Stacking

Prosecutorial charging power magnifies every structural constraint already described. Exposure to stacked charges, guideline enhancements, and mandatory minimums creates a risk calculus that overwhelmingly disfavors trial. Defendants are warned by counsel, often accurately, that exercising the right to trial may result in dramatically harsher punishment. The warning is not rhetorical. It is embedded in charging decisions and sentencing structures that escalate exposure before a jury ever hears the case.

Charge stacking converts prosecutorial discretion into coercive leverage. By layering counts, enhancements, and statutory triggers, prosecutors can manufacture sentencing ranges that bear little relationship to culpability while exerting decisive control over outcomes. The resulting decision making is not shared. It is imposed. The question is no longer whether the government can prove its case, but whether the defendant is willing to risk catastrophic punishment to demand that proof. What is presented as choice is, in reality, calibrated fear.

At that point, the process is no longer oriented toward justice being served. It is oriented toward the prosecution prevailing. Charging authority that is nominally justified as a means of protecting the public is pushed far beyond that purpose. Punishment is no longer tethered to public safety or proportional accountability. It becomes a tool for enforcing compliance and securing convictions. The severity of exposure is not calibrated to risk posed by the defendant, but to resistance shown by the defendant.

Counsel advising caution under these conditions is not acting irrationally. They are responding to a system designed to make resistance costly. But the rationality of that advice exposes the constitutional problem rather than resolving it. When the exercise of a constitutional right triggers punishment untethered from the underlying offense, the adversarial process ceases to function as a mechanism for truth or justice. It becomes a mechanism for outcome control.

The leverage depends on cooperation by the defendant. Cooperation to plead. Cooperation to waive trial. Cooperation to narrow issues. Cooperation to preserve efficiency. When cooperation is withheld, punishment escalates. When it is given, exposure recedes. This is not incidental. It is how the system signals which conduct it rewards and which it punishes.

The trial penalty reshapes defense advocacy itself. Investigation is curtailed because trial is treated as unlikely. Motions are constrained because challenging the government risks worsening exposure. Strategic decisions are filtered through fear of retaliation rather than assessment of merit. Defense advocacy narrows, not because defenses are unavailable, but because asserting them carries a price that the system has made irrational to pay.

Charge stacking and mandatory minimums thus operate as enforcement tools against the exercise of constitutional rights. They do not prohibit trial. They price it out of reach. When insisting on adjudication invites punishment rather than judgment, the Sixth Amendment no longer functions as a guarantee. It functions as a warning. The right remains nominally intact, but the cost of invoking it ensures that plea is the only rational response.

Discovery Leverage and Time Pressure

Discovery asymmetry compounds every imbalance already described. Defendants often receive discovery late, in fragmented form, or under conditions that make meaningful review difficult. Production may arrive in waves, without organization, without indexing, and without context. Critical materials are buried in volume, produced close to deadlines, or disclosed only after strategic decisions have already been forced.

Motions to compel, suppress, or exclude evidence are theoretically available, but practically constrained. They require time to identify deficiencies, resources to investigate what is missing, and capacity to litigate disputes that indigent defense systems are not structured to absorb. Even where such motions are warranted, they carry institutional risk, as funding requests are frequently denied and discovery disputes are discouraged rather than supported.

Deadlines continue to run regardless of readiness. Speedy trial clocks advance. Plea offers expire. Sentencing exposure hardens. The pressure to resolve intensifies not because the case has been fully evaluated, but because the system continues to move forward on a schedule that assumes defense readiness that does not exist. Time itself becomes leverage.

Discovery delay functions as a strategic advantage even without formal dispute resolution. The government need not prevail on the merits of a discovery dispute to benefit from it. Delay alone is sufficient. Each postponement compresses the window for investigation, limits the ability to file meaningful motions, and increases the cost of insisting on adjudication. By the time discovery can be fully reviewed, the consequences of proceeding to trial have already escalated.

Counsel advising a plea under these conditions is fully aware that guilt will be conceded. What drives that advice is not a determination that the government's case has been tested and proven, but recognition that the prosecution has structured the process to make meaningful testing prohibitively dangerous. The plea becomes a mechanism for damage control in a system where the AUSA's objective is no longer justice, but prevailing at any cost.

This system carries extraordinary human cost. It routinely converts cases that might warrant two or three years of punishment into sentences of ten, twenty, or thirty years. These outcomes are not reserved for violent conduct. They frequently attach to non-violent offenses, often involving first-time defendants, where exposure is driven less by harm than by leverage, delay, and prosecutorial escalation.

This pressure reshapes the adversarial process. Discovery is no longer a tool for testing the government's case. It becomes a countdown. Each disclosure arrives not as an opportunity to challenge, but as a reminder that the window for doing so is closing. The right to confront evidence exists in theory while evaporating in practice.

Discovery leverage and time pressure thus work together to manufacture urgency. Resolution is framed as prudence. Delay is framed as recklessness. The system does not wait for defense readiness. It advances until resistance becomes irrational. By the time discovery is complete, the plea decision has already been structurally compelled in service of winning, not justice.

Engineered Surrender

Indigent defendants are not situated to litigate on equal terms. Counsel is appointed late. Funding is minimal. Investigation and motion practice are discouraged rather than supported. Exposure is inflated through charge stacking and mandatory minimums. Defendants are warned about trial penalties, denied meaningful discovery leverage, and forced to operate under time and resource constraints that they did not create and cannot control.

Within this architecture, plea bargaining is not a choice made after adversarial testing. It is the only rational exit available. When the system boasts of high plea rates, it is not describing efficiency. It is describing engineered surrender.

These outcomes are later cited as proof that the system works. Dockets move. Convictions are secured. Metrics are satisfied. The government gets its win. What disappears from view is not only whether the defendant ever had a realistic opportunity to contest the case, but whether the question of guilt was ever meaningfully tested at all.

This is not justice administered efficiently. It is resolution extracted under conditions deliberately structured to make resistance irrational. Pressure substitutes for proof. Speed substitutes for fairness. Waiver substitutes for adjudication.

The Sixth Amendment promises the right to counsel and the right to trial. For indigent defendants, those rights exist formally, while the surrounding architecture ensures they are rarely exercised. The system does not forbid trial. It renders it unusable.

That distinction matters. A system that measures success by how quickly cases end or arrive at a plea is not evaluating justice or truth. It is measuring how effectively surrender has been engineered, including in cases where the defendant may not be guilty at all. When guilt is never tested and innocence is never examined, convictions become engineered pressure rather than determinations of fact.

Plea Rates as Institutional Performance Metrics

Conviction rates routinely exceeding ninety percent are often cited as evidence of system effectiveness and government competence. They are presented as proof that cases are handled efficiently, that charging decisions are sound, and that outcomes are reliable. In reality, these figures do not measure accuracy, fairness, or prosecutorial merit. They measure how successfully cases are disposed of without ever being meaningfully tested.

High plea rates are not organic outcomes. They are produced by containment mechanisms operating long before a jury is empaneled.

Chronic underfunding of defense, asymmetrical charging power, discovery leverage, trial penalties, and institutional impatience with litigation converge to narrow defendants' options until pleading becomes the only rational response. The metric records the endpoint of that process, not the legitimacy of what preceded it.

When institutions invoke plea rates to demonstrate competence, they invert the constitutional inquiry. The question is no longer whether guilt was established through adversarial proof, but how quickly the case was disposed of. Adjudication is treated as waste. Time spent litigating is treated as failure. Assertion of rights is treated as noncompliance with expectations of cooperation, efficiency, and early resolution rather than as constitutional engagement.

These metrics reward speed over scrutiny. They privilege resolution over evidentiary development. They incentivize practices that compress timelines, discourage motion practice, and penalize defendants who insist on building a record. The system adapts to what it measures. When closure becomes the benchmark, pressure becomes policy.

Most importantly, plea rates erase the distinction between guilt and compliance. A plea is counted the same whether it follows rigorous adversarial development or whether it is entered under conditions that make contest impossible. The metric does not capture innocence, imbalance, or distortion. It captures only submission.

These are not flattering numbers. They do not reflect prosecutorial strength or system integrity. They reflect how effectively adjudication has been displaced by pressure and coercion. They demonstrate how thoroughly adjudication has been replaced by managed outcomes. When institutional success is defined by how few cases reach trial, the Sixth Amendment is not enforced as a living guarantee. It is reduced to a procedural formality, satisfied on paper while emptied of its function. No institutional pride should be taken in that outcome.

The Human Cost of Economic Design

For indigent defendants, this system communicates a clear message: representation is treated as a favor rather than a right; trial is framed as a hazard rather than a guarantee; acting as an adversary to the government is recast as irresponsibility. The architecture signals that constitutional assertion is disruptive, while compliance is rewarded. The law speaks in the language of rights, but the system operates in the language of tolerance. It will not tolerate an adversarial system that insists on testing its claims.

Humanity is extended generously to institutions. Prosecutors are afforded discretion in the name of efficiency. Courts are granted patience in the name of docket management. Administrative constraints are treated as mitigating realities. But the accused, navigating a system deliberately calibrated against them, are expected to absorb the full weight of consequence without corresponding consideration of imbalance. Their fear is treated as calculation. Their hesitation is treated as defiance. Their insistence on process is treated as obstruction rather than constitutional participation.

The cost of this design is not abstract. It is measured in years of lost liberty, fractured families, economic ruin, and permanent legal stigma. It is borne disproportionately by individuals accused of non-violent conduct, often for the first time, whose exposure escalates not because of danger posed, but because of leverage applied. The system's efficiency is purchased with human life years, extracted through pressure rather than adjudication.

Over time, these outcomes reshape expectations. Defendants learn that asserting rights invites punishment. Counsel learns that challenging the system invites resistance. Courts learn to equate quiet dockets with justice achieved. What begins as structural constraint hardens into cultural norm. Surrender becomes rational. Silence becomes prudent. Pleas become survival, because the cost of liberty is made higher than the cost of surrender.

The result is not merely unequal outcomes. A system that conditions mercy on compliance and imposes punishment for the exertion of constitutional rights does not merely fail to protect constitutional rights. It teaches those subjected to it that their rights were never meant to be used at all. It is the normalization of surrender as justice.

What This Chapter Establishes

This chapter establishes that what appears as failure of indigent defense is not primarily a failure of effort, competence, or commitment. It is the visible consequence of upstream choices that determine whether the Sixth Amendment can function before representation ever begins.

By the time counsel is appointed, the constitutional field has already been narrowed. Resource constraints, procedural compression, and institutional expectations define what defense work can meaningfully occur. Representation does not operate in an open adversarial space. It operates inside boundaries that determine, in advance, which failures will be tolerated and which will never be examined.

What follows is not a breakdown in individual lawyering, but the predictable result of a system that treats appointment as satisfaction and treats enforcement as optional. The Sixth Amendment has not been defeated by argument. It has been hollowed out by design.

Chapter 5
From Indigent Defense to Structural Design

From Representation Failure to Structural Design

This book began with indigent defense because that is where constitutional failure is most visible.

For indigent defendants, the Sixth Amendment is not an abstraction. It is encountered at the point of appointment, under conditions of scarcity, constraint, and imbalance that are impossible to ignore. Representation arrives already shaped by limited time, limited resources, and limited institutional tolerance. The effects are concrete. Investigation narrows. Strategy contracts. Adversarial testing weakens. What should be contested often is not.

This visibility has shaped how Sixth Amendment failure is commonly understood. The focus settles on representation. On counsel performance. On adequacy measured case by case. Failure appears local, personal, and correctable through better lawyering or additional resources.

That appearance is misleading.

Indigent defense is not where the failure originates. It is where the failure concentrates.

The conditions that distort representation are produced upstream, long before any individual lawyer enters a case. Appointment systems, funding structures, charging practices, discretionary thresholds, and tolerance for imbalance determine what defense can realistically look like before strategy is ever formed. By the time representation begins, the range of possible outcomes has already narrowed.

What appears as a breakdown in defense is the downstream expression of structural choice.

This is why the analysis in this book was forced beyond representation. Following the Sixth Amendment honestly required moving upstream, into the design of the system that governs whether constitutional violations are enforced in the system at all. The question could not remain whether counsel performed adequately. It had to become whether the system is structured to permit adjudication to occur.

That inquiry leads inevitably to discretion.

Discretion determines which violations receive attention and which are absorbed. It governs whether error compels response or can be tolerated. It allows constitutional failure to be acknowledged without consequence, corrected without recalibration, or ignored without denial. Discretion is not an aberration in the system. It is one of its primary operating principles.

From discretion, the analysis moves to finality.

Finality governs when inquiry must stop, regardless of what remains unresolved. It converts endurance into legitimacy and closure into proof. Once finality attaches, the question is no longer whether the Sixth Amendment was honored, but whether the judgment can be treated as settled. At that point, enforcement is no longer the objective. Preservation is.

Jurisdiction completes the structure.

By dividing authority across courts and procedural stages, the system permits Sixth Amendment claims to move without ever being adjudicated. Responsibility is deferred rather than denied. Claims are acknowledged as existing and then routed away from decision. What disappears is not the right, but the obligation to enforce it.

These mechanisms do not operate independently. They work together:

Discretion determines whether a violation will be confronted. Finality determines when confrontation must end. Jurisdiction determines whether any forum must decide at all.

The combined effect is a system in which the Sixth Amendment remains visible in language while its enforcement is contingent on discretion, timing, jurisdictional acceptance, and the system's tolerance for disruption.

Indigent defendants bear the consequences of this design more consistently than anyone else. Not because they are uniquely affected by constitutional failure, but because they lack insulation from it. They have no discretionary buffer, no institutional credibility, and no structural margin for error. Where the system permits tolerance of failure, indigent defendants absorb it.

This is why indigent defense remains central to the book even as the analysis turns structural. It is the impact zone. It is where the system's design choices land with the least resistance and the greatest force. But it is not the cause.

The Sixth Amendment is the thread that connects these truths.

It begins as a promise of adversarial testing.
It appears to be satisfied through appointment.
It is weakened through discretion.
It is insulated through finality.
It disappears through non-adjudication.

At no point is the Sixth Amendment formally rejected. Its enforcement is contingent on whether adjudication is permitted to occur at all.

This chapter exists to name that movement explicitly.

What began as an examination of indigent defense could not remain there without becoming inaccurate. Indigent defense reveals the failure. Structure produces it.

The Sixth Amendment does not fail by accident. It fails because enforcement is optional by design. Optional in the sense that it is invoked when it stabilizes outcomes, deferred when it threatens them, and abandoned when adjudication would require disruption the system has decided not to tolerate.

Optional enforcement is indistinguishable from no enforcement at all.

Chapter 6
Post-Conviction Review and the Closed Loop

Convicted Without Adjudication

This chapter examines what follows when criminal cases conclude without meaningful adjudication of guilt or innocence. The failure identified in prior chapters does not end at case resolution. It travels forward, shaping how outcomes are understood, enforced, and lived. Whether a case ends in a plea or proceeds to trial, the system moves on as though guilt has been determined, even when the adversarial process never meaningfully operated.

The central irony is this: an indigent defendant can endure the full spectacle of trial and still never have had a meaningful day in court. The system preserves the theater of adjudication while denying its substance, then treats the resulting conviction as morally final. Guilt is assumed, legitimacy is declared, and the absence of real adversarial testing is quietly erased. **What disappears with it is due process itself**.

Post-conviction review assumes that Sixth Amendment violations can be corrected later. The structure of review ensures that this assumption is rarely tested. Once a conviction is entered, the system proceeds as though any failure in adversarial testing has already been resolved, even when it never occurred. The promise of later correction becomes a substitute for enforcement, not its fulfillment.

Jurisdiction as Deferral, Not Review

Post-conviction procedures assume that constitutional violations can be corrected later. Jurisdictional rules ensure that they rarely are. Jurisdiction does not operate here as a neutral allocation of authority. It operates as a method of deferral, allowing Sixth Amendment claims to be acknowledged without ever being adjudicated.

The Fiction of Having Had One's Day in Court

The criminal justice system rests on a powerful assumption: that the existence of procedure is equivalent to a fair trial. If hearings were held, motions were filed, and a trial date appeared on the docket, the system treats the outcome as legitimate. But the presence of process does not mean a defendant actually had their day in court. A fair trial requires meaningful adversarial engagement. And for indigent defendants, that engagement is often absent regardless of how formally complete the proceedings appear.

Formal compliance is not the same as a fair contest. A case can move from indictment to resolution with every procedural box checked and still never meaningfully confront the substance of the government's allegations. Evidence may go unchallenged not because it is sound, but because the defense lacked the time, resources, or institutional tolerance to test it. Strategy may be narrowed not by judgment, but by constraint. What survives is the appearance of fairness, not its reality.

Over time, these constraints reshape defense advocacy itself. Counsel learn which requests will be denied, which experts will not be funded, and which motions will be discouraged or ignored. As a result of this conditioning, counsel makes a calculated decision not to ask for relief that effective representation would otherwise require. But the failure to ask does more than limit defense strategy. It prevents the development of a record. When investigative needs are not formally asserted and evidentiary challenges are never raised, the absence of litigation is later treated as proof that nothing was required.

This failure is not confined to cases resolved by plea. An indigent defendant can proceed to trial and still never receive a meaningful day in court. A jury does not cure a hollow defense. A verdict does not supply fairness when investigation was truncated, motions were never pursued, and adversarial engagement was constrained long before opening statements began. The presence of a jury preserves the form of a fair trial, not its substance.

The system nevertheless treats outcomes produced under these conditions as conclusive. Convictions are accepted as legitimate not because a fair trial occurred, but because the process appeared complete. The inquiry stops at procedure. Whether the defendant ever received a real opportunity to contest the case is never asked.

This is the fiction:
That a defendant who passed through the machinery must have
had their day in court.

When Trial Preserves Form but Denies Substance

The existence of a trial is treated as the system's final proof of fairness.
Once a jury is seated and a verdict returned, the process is assumed
to have done its work. But a trial is not meaningful simply because
it occurred. When the defense never had the ability to function as
an adversary to the government, the trial becomes something else
entirely. It becomes a performance.

Everyone plays their role.

The courtroom is activated. The government presents its case with
the benefit of investigation, continuity, and institutional authority.
The judge manages the proceeding. The jury listens. The defense
speaks when called upon. From the outside, the process appears
complete. Inside, the imbalance that shaped the case long before
trial remains untouched.

Indigent defendants routinely reach trial without the conditions
that are necessary to make the trial real. Investigation is incomplete
or never undertaken. Experts are not retained. Alternative theories
are not developed. Suppression issues are missed, abandoned, or
never raised. The government's evidence goes largely untested, not
because it is unassailable, but because the defense lacked the time,
funding, and institutional tolerance to challenge it. By the time the

jury is sworn, the defense is not presenting a considered strategy. It is presenting what remains after constraint has already done its work.

What occurs in these trials is not adversarial testing. It is containment.

The government's narrative arrives intact. The defense response arrives narrowed, incomplete, and reactive. This imbalance is not the product of choices made in the courtroom. It is structural. It cannot be corrected at trial because it was created before trial ever began.

Once a trial has occurred, courts treat the proceeding as complete. There is no further inquiry into whether the defense had the capacity to function as an adversary. The verdict itself is taken as confirmation that the process worked. The existence of trial is treated as proof of fairness, rather than as something that might itself require examination.

This is where the substitution occurs.

The presence of a jury is allowed to substitute for the presence of a constitutionally sufficient defense.

From that point forward, the substance of what actually happened in the courtroom no longer matters. The verdict closes the question. The imbalance that shaped the trial disappears from view, replaced by the assumption that guilt was established through a fair process.

And once the verdict is entered, inquiry ends. The outcome is treated as final not because the case was truly tested, but because the performance was completed. The machinery moves forward as though truth were determined, even when the conditions required to determine it never existed.

Form survives. Substance disappears. And the conviction that follows is treated as morally complete, not because guilt was established, but because the system succeeded in making it look like it was.

Public Narrative and Moral Finality

Once a conviction is entered, the system does not merely record an outcome. It announces the appearance of a settled truth. What may have been unresolved, constrained, or never meaningfully tested inside the courtroom is immediately translated into public certainty outside of it. The internal limits of the process disappear, replaced by a narrative of accountability, closure, and justice.

Prosecutorial statements play a central role in this translation. Press releases and interviews speak in the language of resolution. Defendants are described as having been "held accountable." Victims are told that justice has been done. The case is framed as concluded, the facts as established, and the outcome as deserved. The conviction is presented as confirmation of guilt, even though it is only the result of a process that, had it functioned properly, could have yielded a not guilty result. No distinction is drawn between proof that was tested and proof that was assumed.

Media coverage reinforces this framing. Reports rely heavily on official accounts and courtroom outcomes, not on the conditions under which those outcomes were produced. Trials are reported as proof of fairness. Verdicts are reported as determinations of truth.

The appearance of procedure substitutes for inquiry. What is missing from the story is not neutrality, but instead, the truth about how these outcomes are manufactured. The constraints that shaped the defense never appear. The imbalance that governed the trial is invisible to the public record.

This narrative does not require bad faith to function. It requires closure. Conviction is treated as a moral resolution because the system requires outcomes to appear settled in order to move forward. There is no space in the public narrative for uncertainty, constraint, or structural failure. Those concepts threaten the legitimacy of outcomes that the system has already decided to preserve.

Over time, this framing hardens into assumption. Guilt is treated not as something that was proven through a functioning adversarial process, but as something established by the fact of the conviction itself. Questions about how the case was handled are reframed as excuses. Concerns about the quality of defense are dismissed as dissatisfaction with losing. The conviction becomes self-validating, and the process that produced it recedes from view.

This is how internal failure becomes external certainty. A system that may never have meaningfully tested guilt still produces outcomes that must be treated as if guilt were established. The public is not invited to ask whether the defense functioned, whether evidence was challenged, or whether the trial could have ended differently under fair conditions. The verdict answers all questions by ending them.

Moral finality does more than justify punishment. It insulates the system from scrutiny. Once guilt is treated as settled truth, any challenge to the process is treated as an attack on justice itself. The possibility that the outcome is contingent, rather than conclusive, is erased. What remains is confidence without examination.

Second-Class Citizenship

People marked by conviction are barred from ordinary forms of participation that define full citizenship. They are prohibited from coaching Little League teams, from chaperoning school trips, from volunteering in classrooms where their own children sit. In some states, they are barred from voting, stripped of a political voice as though citizenship itself is conditional. These exclusions are imposed without inquiry into the underlying conduct and without regard to how the conviction was produced. The verdict alone is treated as sufficient proof of unfitness.

Licensing regimes reinforce this status. Professional credentials are denied or revoked automatically. Careers are foreclosed without hearings that examine actual conduct or present capacity. Employment applications require disclosure that functions as a permanent disqualification. Housing opportunities disappear behind background checks that treats the conviction as character. These restrictions do not ask what happened. They ask only whether the system has spoken.

Civil rights follow the same logic. People lose the ability to possess a firearm, not because a current risk has been tested and proven, but because a conviction is treated as a permanent marker of disqualification.

Social stigma completes the process. Conviction becomes identity. Suspicion becomes permanent. Individuals are required to carry the weight of an outcome that was never meaningfully tested into every space they enter. They are expected to live under moral certainty produced by a process that did not function as an adversarial one nor a fair contest.

This is not an unintended byproduct of the criminal process. It is a feature of it. These exclusions enforce the system's declaration that guilt is settled and status is permanent. They extend punishment indefinitely, beyond sentence and supervision, without ever asking whether the process that produced the conviction deserved that authority.

People are punished as though guilt was reliably established, even when the process that produced the conviction never functioned as a meaningful adversarial test. Their exclusion is justified not by proof, but by finality. What the courtroom failed to resolve, society enforces anyway.

What This Chapter Establishes

This chapter establishes that Sixth Amendment failure does not remain confined to the courtroom. Once an outcome is produced, that failure is carried forward and enforced elsewhere in indigent defendant's lives.

After conviction, what matters is no longer how the case was built or tested, but that it has been closed. The result is a form of punishment that extends indefinitely and operates beyond the criminal case itself. People are continually punished without proof that guilt was ever determined in a process capable of determining it.

The next chapter turns to how this condition is preserved. It examines the procedural mechanisms that convert unresolved questions into settled outcomes, and how time, exhaustion, and finality are used to protect closure from challenge.

Chapter 7
Finality as Governance

The previous chapter examined what follows once an outcome is produced. This chapter shows how time, procedure, and exhaustion are used to convert unresolved questions into settled conclusions. It explains how unresolved questions are converted into settled outcomes. Finality does not emerge naturally from accuracy. It is enforced as a governing principle.

When Closure Becomes the Priority

When a criminal case ends, the system's work is not complete. It has only changed shape. The inquiry is no longer whether the outcome was produced through a process capable of honoring the Sixth Amendment's guarantee of meaningful defense. The inquiry becomes whether the case can be treated as finished.

Closure is not neutral. Closure is the goal. A completed case is treated as a correct one, not because the process functioned properly, but because the system has moved past it. Reopening a conviction is framed as disruption rather than examination, as a threat to institutional order rather than an effort to determine whether guilt was ever meaningfully tested.

This shift is most visible in post-conviction proceedings, particularly for indigent defendants. The barriers governing collateral review do not merely preserve closure. They routinely protect flawed processes by insulating them from scrutiny. Presumptions harden not because error has been ruled out, but because revisiting the case would require confronting how often the Sixth Amendment operates as a formality rather than a functioning safeguard.

Post-conviction review begins from the premise that the outcome is correct simply because it exists. Indigent defendants bear the burden of reopening cases that were never structurally capable of producing reliable verdicts in the first place. The system does not ask whether counsel had the time, resources, or capacity to function as an adversary. It asks whether the challenge arrives too late, violates procedural rules, or threatens finality.

This is not a thought experiment. It is a real Supreme Court decision issued in recent years, and its effects are already shaping post-conviction practice. In that case, a federal prisoner became legally innocent only after the Court clarified that the statute under which he had been convicted did not apply to his conduct at all. The legal basis for his conviction did not weaken. It disappeared. His claim of innocence was unavailable at trial and during his first post-conviction challenge because the law itself had not yet been clarified.

When he later attempted to raise that claim, the government did not argue that he was guilty. It argued that he was too late. Because he had already pursued his single authorized post-conviction motion, he was procedurally barred from presenting a claim that the law now recognized as valid. The Court agreed. His innocence did not matter. Liberty yielded to finality.

One is left with the unavoidable question of whether this outcome was ever truly avoidable. The system's answer assumes that errors can be corrected later, but that assumption rests on a fiction. It presumes that an indigent defendant will recognize the legal significance of a future change in law, understand how it applies to his conviction, and possess the knowledge and resources necessary to raise that claim within a system governed by procedural traps. It assumes that someone processed through a constitutionally deficient defense will later emerge as a legal scholar capable of navigating post-conviction procedures. That promise of later correction is not a safeguard. It structures the finality outcome in advance.

The system often repeats the maxim that it is better for the guilty to go free than for the innocent to be punished. That principle is invoked to justify demanding proof, enforcing constitutional protections, and honoring the Sixth Amendment at trial. Yet when finality is threatened, that principle collapses. An innocent person is not merely asked to risk one wrongful day in custody. He is told that innocence itself is irrelevant if it arrives after the system has decided the case is closed.

This is devastating, but it is not accidental. It is not an oversight. It is the consequence of a system in which finality is treated as the governing objective and justice as a contingent one. The same system that tolerates imprecise law, constrained defense, and judicial deference at the front-end refuses to correct those failures once an outcome has hardened.

Once closure takes hold, the system no longer measures legitimacy by the quality of the process or the accuracy of the result. It measures legitimacy by durability. The intended outcome is not justice. It is permanence.

Justice is aspirational. Finality is operational.

Time as a Weapon

Time is treated as neutral only because naming it accurately would expose its function. What is described as delay is more precisely timing, and timing is not incidental to the system. It is one of its primary tools.

At every stage of a criminal case, timing shapes what can be seen, tested, and corrected. Investigations are rushed. Motions are constrained. Trials proceed without full development. Appeals arrive years later, when records have thinned and memory has faded. Post-conviction review comes after the ground has already shifted beneath the defendant's feet.

The system does not merely allow time to pass. It uses timing to avoid work it no longer wants to do: reinvestigating facts, reconstructing records, revisiting credibility, confronting prior error, and reopening judgments that have already been absorbed into finality.

Timing converts unresolved error into presumed correctness.

As time stretches, evidence degrades. Records are lost, destroyed, or deemed unavailable. Witnesses disappear. Memories are discounted. Lawyers change or withdraw. Access to meaningful representation narrows. What once could have been tested becomes impractical to examine. What once demanded adjudication becomes too costly to revisit.

This is the exhaustion of time.

Exhaustion is not limited to emotion or stamina. It is evidentiary, procedural, financial, and cognitive. The defendant bears the full cost of waiting. Resources are depleted. Legal knowledge becomes stale. Procedural windows close. The burden of persistence rests entirely on the individual, while the system incurs no corresponding obligation to move.

Waiting costs the system nothing.
Waiting costs the defendant everything.

Over time, unresolved claims are no longer treated as unresolved. They are treated as settled by endurance. The length of time a judgment has survived begins to substitute for an inquiry into how it was produced. Survival is mistaken for legitimacy.

At that point, the governing objective has shifted. The system is no longer oriented toward letting justice be done. It is oriented toward letting the judgment be final. Those two aims are not synonymous.

Accuracy yields to institutional convenience.
Integrity yields to the maintenance of the process.
Timing insulates the judgment.

Time does not justify the outcome.
It protects it.

Timing is not accidental.
It functions as insulation.

Procedure as Moral Judgment

At a certain point, the system stops evaluating its own performance and starts evaluating the defendant's performance inside of the system. Discretion determines whether the Sixth Amendment operates as a guarantee or as a formality. The right exists regardless of discretion, but enforcement does not. The question quietly shifts. It is no longer whether the conviction was produced through a constitutionally valid process. It becomes why the defendant failed to raise the issue correctly, earlier, and in the proper way.

That shift is not procedural.
It is moral.

Procedure is described as neutral because neutrality conceals judgment. Waiver, default, untimeliness, and successive petition bars are framed as administrative necessities. They are justified as tools for managing cases, preserving finality, and preventing abuse. But once these rules are invoked, procedure stops functioning as case management and begins functioning as attribution.

Claims are dismissed not because they lack constitutional substance, but because they were not raised at the correct moment, in the correct form, through the correct channel. The language is familiar and unforgiving. This should have been raised earlier. You had your opportunity. You cannot raise this now.

What that language obscures is what the system actually provided.

An indigent defendant is guaranteed counsel at trial and on direct appeal. After that, counsel disappears. At post-conviction, the defendant remains indigent, remains incarcerated, and remains subject to the consequences of constitutional error, yet is deemed undeserving of assistance to identify or litigate those errors.

The system demands legal performance without providing legal capacity.

Procedure assumes knowledge that the defendant was never given. It assumes access to legal materials that are often restricted or unavailable. It assumes access to records that may be lost, withheld, or unreachable. It assumes the ability to conduct discovery in a setting where discovery is largely forbidden and where the Bureau of Prisons controls access to documents, communication, and information.

These assumptions are not examined.
Their outcomes are enforced.

When a defendant fails to meet them, the system does not treat that failure as accidental or unfortunate. It treats it as disqualifying and intentional. The failure becomes the justification for refusing to adjudicate the claim at all.

This is where adjudication is quietly abandoned.

Claims are not rejected after being tested. They are barred before they are ever adjudicated. The system treats passage through procedure as a substitute for the constitutional inquiry it declines to perform. The word adjudication is preserved, but its function is not.

Lack of knowledge becomes waiver.
System-imposed delay becomes untimeliness.
Inability to frame claims becomes default.

And persistence becomes abuse.

When a defendant repeatedly raises unresolved constitutional violations that have never been adjudicated on their merits, that effort is no longer understood as an attempt to secure review. It is recast as misuse of the process. Repetition becomes bad faith. Insistence becomes harassment.

The conclusion is unmistakable.

This is moral judgment because the system is no longer deciding whether a constitutional violation occurred. It is deciding whether the defendant deserves to be heard at all. The focus shifts from legality to worthiness. From compliance with the Constitution to compliance with the process. From justice to behavior.

You did not fail because the system malfunctioned.
You failed because you did not survive it correctly.

That is how procedure becomes judgment.
And judgment becomes finality.

Participation Without Capacity

The system requires defendants to participate in a series of prescribed procedures if they want relief. Participation is mandatory. Failure to participate is treated as forfeiture. What is not disclosed is that participation does not guarantee effectiveness.

This is not because the system lacks procedures.
It is because those procedures are not designed to yield correction for the defendant.

This design means that the harm isn't accidental, personal, or fixable by better intentions from the defendant. It is architectural.

An opportunity is not defined by whether a claim could be resolved. It is defined by whether the defendant was permitted to move through a required step. Opportunity is measured by formal access to a procedure, not by whether that procedure is structured to produce a meaningful result.

This is how opportunity comes to substitute for outcome. Availability replaces effectiveness.

To understand this, the procedures must be described as they actually operate.

A criminal case begins at trial. Many constitutional violations occur here, but they are not always visible at the time. Failures to investigate, undisclosed conflicts of interest, suppressed evidence, and misconduct outside the courtroom often leave no trace in the trial record. The defendant is represented, but has no practical ability to identify or preserve these violations while the case is unfolding.

Next comes direct appeal. On appeal, defendants are represented by counsel, and constitutional claims are recognized as such. But appellate review is confined to the trial record. If a constitutional violation depends on facts outside of that record, the appellate court cannot examine it. The claim is acknowledged as constitutional and then deferred. It is redirected to a later stage.

That later stage is post-conviction review. This is where claims that could not be addressed on appeal are supposed to be resolved. But this is also where representation disappears. Counsel is no longer guaranteed. The very claims that were identified as constitutional are now assigned to an incarcerated, indigent defendant proceeding alone.

What could have been investigated and developed with counsel earlier is now required to be proven without the tools necessary to prove it. Subpoena power is absent. Discovery is discretionary and frequently denied. Access to records is incomplete or unavailable. The system demands evidence while withholding access to the very materials that would generate it.

The resulting lack of evidence is then treated as a failure of proof. What is never acknowledged is that this absence was produced by the structure itself. Discretion is used to deny discovery, and the resulting lack of evidence is later cited as the reason relief fails.

After post-conviction review comes habeas review, which insulates the outcome further. At this stage, the inquiry shifts. The question is no longer whether a constitutional violation occurred. It is whether earlier handling of the claim was unreasonable under deferential standards. The focus moves away from accuracy and toward preservation. The judgment becomes insulated from challenge, not because its correctness has been established, but because undoing it would disrupt finality.

This is the insulation that matters.
Not insulation of guilt, but insulation of the judgment.

Alongside these judicial procedures are mechanisms for raising concerns about counsel and misconduct. These include hearings such as Marsden-type proceedings and other judicial review processes. Courts have the authority to compel testimony. They have the authority to order discovery. They have the authority to investigate claims of ineffective assistance, conflicts, and misconduct.

The problem is not the absence of authority.
It is the decision not to use it.

Complaints are processed rather than examined. Issues are acknowledged without being resolved. The existence of a mechanism is treated as sufficient, even when that mechanism is not used to determine the truth of the claim.

Finally, the system enforces procedural bars such as waiver, default, untimeliness, and restrictions on successive filings. These bars do not ask whether a claim was ever adjudicated on the merits. They ask whether the defendant navigated the sequence correctly. Waiver does not mean that a defendant knowingly gave up a right. It means that a claim was not raised at an earlier stage, even when the structure of that stage made it impossible to raise it meaningfully. Silence produced by lack of access, lack of counsel, or lack of information is later treated as choice.

A claim may be adjudicated in the sense that it was processed and denied, without ever being adjudicated on its merits.

Only one of those determines whether a constitutional violation actually occurred.

This design is not created to yield results for the defendant. It is created to move claims forward until they no longer threaten the judgment. Participation is required. Effectiveness is optional. Correction is not the objective.

By the time the sequence is complete, the system no longer asks whether the conviction was constitutionally obtained. It asks only whether the process was followed.

The system does not ask whether justice was done.
It asks whether participation occurred.

Participation without effectiveness is not access.
It is how finality is manufactured.

Finality as Legitimacy

At the end of the sequence, finality no longer functions as an end-point. It functions as proof.

Once a case is closed, closure itself becomes evidence. The system stops asking whether the outcome was produced through a process capable of determining truth and begins treating the fact that the case is over as confirmation that it must be right. A closed case is assumed to be a correct case. Stability substitutes for truth. Completion substitutes for justification.

This is not an accident of time. It is how legitimacy is manufactured.

Earlier stages still speak the language of correction. There are procedures, standards, and statutes that appear to exist for identifying error. But as a case moves forward, the objective quietly changes. What matters is no longer how the decision was reached, but that it has been reached and secured. The longer an outcome remains undisturbed, the more it is treated as settled reality rather than a conclusion that must continue to earn its authority.

Finality does not merely end inquiry. It ends the obligation to explain.

Reopening a case is therefore not treated as a return to truth testing. It is treated as a disruption. The threat is not that a constitutional violation may have occurred, but that the system may have to admit that its earlier confidence was misplaced. Error becomes secondary. Stability becomes paramount.

This is where legitimacy detaches from accuracy.

Once finality attaches, the outcome no longer needs to be defended on the merits. It only needs to be protected. Time itself begins to do the work that evidence once did. The passage of years becomes a substitute for proof. Closure becomes a credential the system points to when it no longer wishes to look behind the result.

At this stage, legitimacy no longer depends on whether guilt was meaningfully tested. It depends on endurance. If the outcome has survived long enough, it is treated as having earned its authority, regardless of how it was produced.

This is how Sixth Amendment failure becomes self-sealing. When adjudication is constrained, incomplete, or distorted, finality does not expose the weakness. It conceals it. The system does not revisit the failure. It absorbs it and moves on, carrying the unresolved error forward as settled truth.

Finality is not neutral here. It is doing active work. It preserves the appearance of justice without requiring justice to have occurred. The case is no longer legitimate because it was decided correctly. It is legitimate because it is finished.

That is what finality legitimizes.

And that is why reopening is treated not as an opportunity to correct constitutional failure, but as a threat to the system's claim that it functioned as it was supposed to. Closure is no longer a preference. It is the condition on which legitimacy now depends.

This is where the chapter's title finally becomes unavoidable.

Finality is not just the end of the case.

It is the proof the system relies on when it no longer wants to look any closer.

What This Chapter Establishes

This chapter establishes that finality is not passive and it is not neutral. It is enforced.

Finality governs which questions may still be asked and which must remain unanswered. Once it takes hold, the system's burden changes. The outcome no longer needs to be examined, justified, or tested. It only needs to be preserved.

This chapter shows how time, procedure, discretion, and compelled participation work together to convert unresolved constitutional failure into settled legitimacy. What was never fully tested is treated as conclusively resolved, not because it was proven, but because it endured.

The next chapter turns to how this condition is maintained. Not by answering unresolved questions, but by ensuring they can no longer be meaningfully raised.

Chapter 8
Jurisdictional Deflection and Non-Adjudication

Jurisdictional Deflection and Non-Adjudication

Appellate review also operates through jurisdictional segmentation that allows constitutional claims to disappear without ever being resolved. Authority is divided in a way that permits each court to decline responsibility while the claim remains unanswered. Trial courts refuse to address claims they characterize as belonging to appellate authority. Appellate courts decline to address claims by invoking procedural posture, waiver, or the availability of collateral review. The claim moves between forums, but it is never decided.

Jurisdiction is one of the primary means by which Sixth Amendment enforcement disappears without being denied. Claims are acknowledged as existing, referenced as procedural history, and then routed until no forum is required to decide them. What vanishes is not the claim itself, but the obligation to adjudicate it.

This structure creates a gap in adjudication. A defendant may raise a constitutional claim regarding the denial of counsel at the appellate stage, only to be told that the trial court lacks authority to review appellate decisions. When that same claim is later raised on appeal from post-conviction proceedings, it may again go unaddressed, absorbed into the general affirmation of denial without direct engagement. At no point is the constitutional question confronted on its merits.

The result is not an adverse ruling. It is something more corrosive. The claim is acknowledged as existing, referenced as procedural history, and then set aside. Jurisdiction becomes the mechanism by which enforcement is avoided without ever being openly denied.

This pattern reinforces finality while preserving institutional boundaries. Each court respects the limits of its authority. Each defers to the other. No court accepts responsibility for resolving the constitutional question, even though courts are obligated to adjudicate the claims properly before them. The judgment remains intact not because the claim lacked merit, but because no forum accepted the obligation to decide it.

What appears as institutional restraint thus operates as constitutional evasion. The structure permits courts to preserve legitimacy, maintain finality, and avoid confrontation, all while a claim that required adjudication remains unanswered. For the indigent defendant, this means the loss of constitutional protection without the benefit of a ruling, a record, or meaningful review. The claim disappears, the judgment hardens, and the defendant bears the full consequence of a system that declined to decide what it was required to adjudicate. What is lost in this process is not merely relief, but the Sixth Amendment's demand for adjudication.

The Effect of Non-Adjudication

Non-adjudication is not neutral. When a constitutional claim is never resolved, the absence of a ruling is later treated as the absence of error. Silence functions as denial. The failure to decide becomes evidence that nothing required decision.

This transformation is structural. Once a claim passes through review without adjudication, its unresolved status is converted into a presumption of correctness. Later courts reference the absence of findings as confirmation that no violation occurred, even when that absence exists precisely because no court accepted responsibility for deciding the claim. What was never addressed is later understood as having been rejected.

This is how appellate review preserves finality while maintaining the appearance of constitutional consideration. Appellate orders recite governing standards. Courts emphasize restraint. Jurisdictional limits are invoked as explanations rather than barriers. The process appears complete, even though the core constitutional claim remains untouched.

At this stage, the indigent defendant is often proceeding pro se. Appellate counsel has withdrawn or substitute counsel has been denied, and the defendant is left to navigate a procedural landscape that presumes legal expertise. The failure to adjudicate the claim is compounded by the defendant's lack of access to counsel capable of identifying, framing, and preserving constitutional issues in the precise manner that courts require.

Non-adjudication then interacts with timing rules to foreclose enforcement entirely. As the claim moves through procedural stages without resolution, statutory and rule-based deadlines continue to run. When the defendant later attempts to raise the unresolved constitutional issue, courts respond not by addressing the substance of the claim, but by invoking timeliness. The claim is dismissed not because it lacked merit, but because the clock expired while it remained undecided. A claim cannot expire while it remains unresolved. The indigent defendant does not know this. The system does. Yet the system proceeds.

In some cases, the foreclosure is complete from the outset. Certain constitutional claims may be raised only through post-conviction proceedings in the first instance. For example, a claim challenging the denial of appellate counsel in their direct appeal or the failure to appoint substitute counsel must be presented through a § 2255 motion before it can be reviewed anywhere else. When such a claim is timely presented and the district court declines to adjudicate it on the ground that authority lies with the appellate court, there is no alternative forum for the defendant to turn to.

The claim cannot be rerouted by the litigant, particularly where the defendant is proceeding pro se. Certification, clarification, or referral between courts are judicial functions, not tools available to indigent defendants. When the district court neither adjudicates the claim nor facilitates its proper routing, the only authorized avenue for presentation is closed. Finality may still attach, but it does so not because the claim was resolved, but because the system declined to decide it.

In some instances, the appellate court does not correct this failure, but affirms it. Rather than addressing the absence of adjudication, the appellate court affirms the district court's conclusion that it lacked authority to decide the claim. This resolves the question of jurisdiction while leaving the constitutional claim itself untouched. The appellate court does not identify an alternative forum, does not remand for adjudication, and does not accept responsibility for resolving the claim. The case is closed through affirmation of non-decision rather than constitutional ruling.

Appellate courts often justify this posture by invoking their role as courts of review rather than courts of first instance. In that framing, the appellate court reviews the district court's jurisdictional conclusion and declines to reach issues that were never adjudicated below. But this distinction cannot resolve the problem presented here. Where a constitutional claim was timely raised in the only authorized forum, and the district court declined to adjudicate it, appellate review cannot end with affirmation of abstention. The appellate court may not decide the claim in the first instance, but it retains the obligation to ensure that adjudication occurs somewhere.

Procedural closure may still follow. The Supreme Court may deny certiorari from post-conviction proceedings, bringing formal review to an end without addressing the unresolved constitutional claim. The Court has consistently stated that it is not a court of correction and does not exist to remedy every error. A denial of certiorari therefore carries no implication regarding the merits of the claims presented. It reflects only the Court's discretionary decision not to intervene.

That limitation does not cure the absence of adjudication below. When lower courts have declined to decide a constitutional claim on jurisdictional grounds, the Supreme Court's refusal to grant certiorari does not supply the missing decision. It merely marks the exhaustion of discretionary review. The constitutional question remains unanswered, not because it was resolved, but because no court accepted responsibility for resolving it.

What is lost is not simply relief. What is lost is adjudication itself. The constitutional question is never answered. The obligation to decide is displaced by procedural routing, and enforcement disappears through repetition rather than denial.

For the indigent defendant, the effect is decisive. The claim passes through every available procedural stage without resolution, the record calcifies around silence, and time hardens into finality. The system treats the absence of adjudication as closure, while the underlying constitutional violation remains unexamined.

Where Discretion Disrupts Adjudication

The disruption is not abstract. It occurs at specific, identifiable moments where adjudication should begin and instead is interrupted.

A defendant raises a claim of prosecutorial misconduct or fraud. The claim is specific. It turns on evidence in the government's possession. The defendant requests discovery so that the claim can be supported and tested.

The court refuses discovery as requested.

The court then concludes that there is no evidence to support the claim.

The absence of evidence is treated as a failure of proof, even though the only mechanism by which evidence could be obtained was denied. The conclusion precedes the inquiry. The claim is rejected not because it was examined and disproven, but because it was never allowed to be developed.

This is not adjudication. It is interruption.

The same pattern appears when the government is permitted not to respond. In post-conviction proceedings, the rules require the government to answer each constitutional claim raised. When the court allows the AUSA to bypass that obligation, the process is altered midstream. The adversarial exchange never occurs. The merits of the claim at issue are never joined.

Discretion has entered and displaced adjudication.

The court does not determine whether misconduct occurred. It determines that the claim will not be fully presented. That determination is then treated as if it were a ruling on the merits. Silence is absorbed into the outcome. Finality attaches to what was never answered.

One would expect that allegations of fraud or misconduct by a court officer would trigger heightened scrutiny. They go directly to the integrity of the proceeding itself. If true, they undermine not only the conviction, but the legitimacy of the process that produced it.

Instead, discretion reverses the priority.

Rather than insisting on a complete record, the system accepts incompleteness. Rather than requiring answers, it tolerates omission. The integrity of the proceeding is declared intact precisely because the claim challenging that integrity was never fully adjudicated.

What appears as adjudication is actually foreclosure.

Discretion allows the court to deny without testing, to conclude without inquiry, and to enforce the judgment without ever confronting the constitutional violation alleged. The defendant is faulted for failing to prove what the court refused to allow him to access. The system then proceeds as though the claim has been adjudicated.

This is how discretion disrupts adjudication.

Not by openly rejecting constitutional claims, but by interrupting the process before adjudication can occur, and then treating that interruption as resolution.

Counseled Silence and the Architecture of Finality

The routine appointment of the same counsel to represent a defendant at trial and on direct appeal creates an institutional conflict that structurally limits the exercise of the constitutional right to appeal. Because direct appeal is the only stage at which defendants are guaranteed the assistance of counsel for the review of trial-level error, assigning trial counsel to serve as appellate counsel ensures that the appeal cannot function as a comprehensive review of the proceedings below. Ineffective assistance claims, which necessarily implicate counsel's own performance, are rendered institutionally un-assertable at the appellate stage, not as a matter of law, but as a consequence of role design. This arrangement predictably suppresses a category of constitutional claims at the only point in the process where a defendant is entitled to a full, counseled appeal, allowing procedural finality to attach without the constitutional right to appellate review ever being meaningfully exercised.

The cost of this design is borne entirely by the defendant. When viable constitutional claims are diverted from direct appeal and deferred to post-conviction proceedings, the defendant does not remain in place awaiting adjudication. The defendant's liberty is taken. Time in custody accrues while review is postponed, fragmented, or functionally denied. Even where a claim could ultimately undermine the conviction or sentence, the interim deprivation of freedom is treated as an acceptable byproduct of procedural ordering.

It is often assumed that this conflict is cured by the availability of post-conviction review, because appellate courts routinely direct ineffective assistance claims to proceedings under §2255. But that redirection is a rule of convenience, not a constitutional solution. The existence of a later forum does not restore the right to a full, counseled direct appeal, nor does it replicate the function that direct review is designed to serve. When claims are deferred to post-conviction proceedings as a matter of routine, the system substitutes an uncounseled, structurally constrained process for the very stage at which constitutional review is guaranteed, treating reassignment as equivalence when it is not.

This consequence is often obscured in legal analysis, but it is not theoretical, it is real for the defendant. The redirection of constitutional claims away from the only stage at which defendants are guaranteed counsel does not merely delay review; it converts unresolved constitutional error into lived punishment. The system does not pause the loss of liberty while it decides whether the loss was lawful. It imposes it first, and reviews later, if at all.

How Did We Miss This?

When Review has No Reviewer

A constitutional system cannot pretend that review exists while leaving certain constitutional failures with nowhere to go. Familiarity does not make this condition normal. It makes it structural.

In practice, the federal system operates as if there are two Supreme Courts. One announces constitutional mandates. The other, operating through appellate discretion, jurisdictional routing, and procedural deflection, determines whether those mandates will ever be enforced in individual cases. This is not metaphor. It is an allocation of authority.

When an appellate court renders a constitutional determination that is final as to the litigant, insulated from collateral review, and unlikely to be reviewed by the Supreme Court as a matter of practice, it exercises de facto final constitutional authority. That authority is real, even if it is never named as such. And yet it operates without a corresponding obligation to provide a forum for correction when constitutional error occurs at the appellate stage itself.

Section § 2255 is presented as the primary vehicle for correcting constitutional error. In reality, it is functionally limited to review of the trial court. It provides no meaningful mechanism for adjudicating constitutional violations committed by the appellate court. That limitation becomes acute when the violation involves the denial of counsel on a first appeal as of right.

The right to counsel for example, at that stage is not discretionary. It is mandated by Supreme Court precedent and reinforced by statute. Once a system provides a first appeal as of right, representation is required. The statute does not say counsel may be appointed. It says counsel shall be provided. That language removes discretion entirely.

Yet discretion is routinely substituted for that mandate. Appointed counsel is permitted to withdraw. Substitute counsel is denied. The appeal proceeds with the defendant unrepresented, even though the right to counsel at that stage is clear, settled, and compulsory. When this violation is later raised, there is no forum willing or able to correct it. The appellate court cannot review its own conduct.

Section § 2255 routes the claim back to the district court, which lacks authority to adjudicate constitutional errors committed by the appellate court itself. The Supreme Court, meanwhile, is not structured to function as a court of routine correction for individualized constitutional failures of this kind.

The result is a constitutional violation that is acknowledged in principle but unreachable in practice. The right exists. The mandate exists. The violation occurs. And yet there is no procedural path through which enforcement can occur.

This same displacement appears in other appellate practices that have been normalized without scrutiny. When appellate courts decline to hear ineffective assistance of trial counsel claims on direct appeal, they routinely assert that the record is not developed. That assertion has become formulaic. It is also misleading.

On direct appeal, the appellate court possesses the complete trial record. That record contains the full transcript, all objections and rulings, motions practice, witness examination, and sentencing proceedings. Ineffective assistance of trial counsel arises from that record. Post-conviction proceedings do not retroactively create missing trial facts. They do not add contemporaneous objections. They do not reconstruct adversarial testing that never occurred.

What changes after direct appeal is not the record. What changes is access.

After direct appeal, counsel has withdrawn. The defendant is typically incarcerated. Discovery is restricted or denied. Investigative resources are unavailable. The defendant proceeds pro se. The factual record remains static. Only capacity deteriorates.

When courts invoke the phrase "record not developed," they are not identifying missing facts. They are justifying a rerouting of responsibility. Review is deferred until representation disappears. Enforcement is postponed until it becomes unattainable. Discretion replaces statute. Timing replaces adjudication.

This is how discretion becomes stronger than the rule. Stronger than Supreme Court mandate. Stronger than statutory commands that use the word shall. The law remains intact on paper, but its force is neutralized through procedural design.

The most troubling feature of this structure is not that constitutional violations occur. It is that the system provides no place for them to be heard once they arise at the appellate level. A right without a forum is not a safeguard. It is an abstraction. And when enforcement depends entirely on discretionary willingness rather than mandatory obligation, the absence of correction is not an accident. It is the outcome that the structure produces.

What emerges is not a procedural oversight but an institutional contradiction. The Constitution guarantees review, Congress mandates counsel on a first appeal as of right, and the Supreme Court has declared that mandate binding. Yet appellate courts routinely substitute discretion for obligation, denying counsel where the law requires it and insulating that denial from meaningful correction. The Supreme Court alone holds constitutional finality, but exercises discretionary review. The appellate court lacks that authority, yet controls whether review will ever occur.

The result is a system in which a lower court may nullify a constitutional mandate while no court is compelled to correct it. In that structure, a defendant is left without a forum, without counsel, and without recourse regarding a constitutional right that Congress and the Supreme Court have already guaranteed. Courts routinely acknowledge that relief must exist in principle, while declining to construct an actual procedural path that is capable of delivering it in practice. This design creates a continuing denial of the constitutional issue, where its structure keeps the right trapped in a loop because courts cannot meaningfully review themselves. In essence, the appearance of relief exists, but the path does not.

We should be reminded that: The system does not pause the loss of liberty while the system decides whether the loss was lawful.

Realization Thought:
- If appellate courts refuse constitutional claims on direct appeal
- And §2255 lacks the authority to address Appellate Constitutional Violations
- And the Supreme Court review is discretionary
- And no statute authorizes review of appellate constitutional violations

Then constitutional injury can occur without any court ever having jurisdiction to correct it.

It leaves an unavoidable set of questions lingering:

1. If an appellate court can nullify a constitutional mandate without review, where does constitutional authority actually reside?
2. When discretion overrides mandate and review is optional, is this still a system of constitutional law?

This is where discretion ceased to function as judgment and became a substitute for a constitutional mandate.

What This Chapter Establishes

This chapter establishes that adjudication and adjudicating the merits are not the same thing, and that the federal system routinely treats them as interchangeable once discretion enters.

It shows how constitutional claims can be processed, routed, and resolved without ever being decided. Discretion does not merely manage cases. It deflects claims away from adjudication while preserving the authority of the outcome.

This chapter makes clear that when adjudication is replaced by discretion, the merits do not fail. They are never reached. The system proceeds as though the Constitution has been enforced, even when the claim challenging that enforcement was never addressed.

What remains is not a determination of guilt or innocence, but an enforced conclusion. Finality attaches to what was never adjudicated, and legitimacy is preserved without decision.

The next chapter turns to what happens after this point. Once discretion has deflected adjudication, the system no longer needs to resolve constitutional claims. It only needs to prevent their return.

Chapter 9
When Prosecution Outruns Adjudication & Justice

Purpose of the Chapter

This chapter names the problem that the federal system has refused to confront. It explains how adjudication and justice were displaced, how prosecutorial power became unchecked, and why courts chose accommodation instead of enforcement.

What follows is not about isolated prosecutorial misconduct. It is about how tolerated misconduct reshaped the system itself.

Nobody Notices the Problem

Nobody notices the problem because prosecutorial misconduct is treated as episodic rather than systemic.

Misconduct is visible. Discovery violations are identified. Overcharging is discussed. Implausible conspiracy theories are permitted to proceed. But each instance is processed as a defect within a single case, not as a force that reshapes the system itself. The focus remains narrow. What went wrong here. Whether this particular violation can be addressed. Whether this individual record supports relief.

What is missing is any inquiry into accumulation.

When misconduct is evaluated one case at a time, its broader effects disappear. No single discovery violation appears capable of altering adjudication. No single overcharge appears capable of distorting justice. No single coerced plea appears capable of changing outcomes beyond the defendant who accepted it. Each instance is understood as bounded, contained, and correctable within the four corners of a case.

That framing is what prevents the problem from being seen.

Pleas induced by leverage rather than proof are normalized as efficiency because they are viewed through the lens of individual capacity rather than systemic pressure. Defense counsel is ineffective, overworked, or underfunded. The failure is assigned to representation, not to the charging practices that made effective defense impossible in the first place. The plea resolves the case. The docket moves. The system appears to function.

But what is never examined is how these resolutions, repeated thousands of times, alter the conditions under which adjudication occurs.

The system does not ask what happens when overcharging becomes routine. It does not ask what happens when conspiracy is charged without proof of agreement. It does not ask what happens when preliminary scrutiny disappears, when discovery is restricted, and when defense counsel lacks the time or resources to test the government's case. Each development is addressed, if at all, as a discrete problem with a localized cause.

Because the analysis never widens, the conclusion never changes.

Adjudication and justice are not rejected in law. They are obscured in practice. The Sixth Amendment does not lose its meaning or its force. It remains intact in law. What changes is whether the system creates conditions in which it can be exercised.

The system continues to assume that adjudication remains intact because no single case disproves that assumption on its own. The possibility that repeated prosecutorial misconduct changes outcomes, incentives, and institutional behavior is never fully confronted, not because it is rejected, but because it is never framed as the question.

This is how the damage remains invisible.

Misconduct is acknowledged. Consequences are not. Rights persist on the books while the structure required to vindicate them erodes. The system remains confident in its soundness because it has no mechanism for seeing how the cumulative effect of prosecutorial power reshapes adjudication itself.

This chapter explains that mechanism.

It explains how treating misconduct as episodic prevents the system from recognizing how adjudication and justice are displaced in practice without ever being formally denied. Nothing in this process diminishes constitutional guarantees. What disappears is the system's capacity and willingness to enforce them.

This is the core diagnosis chapter.

It does not catalogue abuses. It explains how repeated, unexamined misconduct transforms the system that absorbs it. It does not assume understanding. It builds it.

What follows names the problem fully, structurally, and without dilution.

Prosecutorial Power as the Central Accelerant

Before examining the consequences, the problem has to be identified precisely. The federal system did not drift into dysfunction accidentally. It changed because one force expanded while all others receded. That force was prosecutorial power.

The criminal justice system did not lose adjudication because adjudication could not work.

It lost adjudication because unrestrained prosecution is incompatible with adjudication, and the courts refused to reassert control when that incompatibility became unavoidable.

This distinction matters.

A system that adjudicates properly does not collapse. We already had one.

The federal system functioned during a period when charging was narrower, conspiracy actually meant agreement, trials were fewer but real, adjudication was expected, appellate correction was routine, and prisons were full but not swollen beyond design. The system did not grind to a halt. It did not become unmanageable. It worked.

What changed was not adjudication.

What changed was the system's tolerance of the prosecution expanding beyond proof, beyond statute, and beyond the system's own capacity to adjudicate.

Federal prosecutors were gradually permitted to charge beyond what the adjudicative structure could sustain. Statutes were stretched beyond their meaning. Conspiracy was untethered from agreement. Enhancements were stacked to create catastrophic exposure. Ordinary conduct was federalized. Threats of extreme sentences became leverage to force pleas.

Once that happened, adjudication became inconvenient.

The problem was never whether courts could adjudicate at that pace. The problem was whether courts were willing to stop prosecutors from creating that pace in the first place.

That is where the system failed.

What followed was not chaos. It was conversion. The judicial system was quietly repurposed into a criminal mill, one in which justice being done was no longer the animating objective. In its place emerged a tolerated equilibrium built around prosecutorial throughput, conviction rates, and career advancement. Winning replaced proving. Closure replaced adjudication. The system did not announce this shift. It normalized it. Courts did not endorse misconduct outright. They accepted its results. Over time, the measure of institutional success ceased to be whether justice had been done and became whether cases were finished and outcomes preserved, because that is all this new acceptance yielded time for.

Deference and discretion, cloaked in prosecutorial familiarity, quietly altered the system from within. What began as professional trust in prosecutorial judgment hardened into institutional permission. Courts did not announce a surrender of oversight. They practiced it. Over time, prosecutors were treated less as advocates subject to constraint and more as internal operators whose judgment could be relied upon without sustained scrutiny. Familiarity dissolved distance. Distance is where accountability lives.

Any system that transfers control from management to its operators changes its incentives. When oversight recedes, self-serving priorities predictably rise. Winning becomes currency. Career advancement becomes metric. Efficiency becomes justification. The mission recedes not because it is rejected, but because it no longer governs daily decision-making. This is not unique to criminal law. It is basic organizational behavior.

The courts confused the authority of the prosecutorial role with the character of the people who occupy it. They treated the position itself as a guarantor of integrity, as though the title transferred restraint, neutrality, and judgment automatically to the individual. But positions do not confer virtue. Uniforms do not eliminate incentives. Power does not cleanse human behavior of ambition, error, or self-interest.

By collapsing the distinction between institutional role and individual conduct, courts allowed discretion to operate without counterweight. That discretion did not remain neutral. It aligned with the incentives it encountered. What else could it do. Over time, prosecutorial familiarity replaced adversarial distance, and oversight gave way to trust. What followed was not isolated misconduct, but systemic drift toward outcomes that rewarded speed, closure, and victory over proof, restraint, and adjudication.

When Misconduct Shapes the Verdict and the Verdict Is Used to Erase the Misconduct

What is never confronted is the obvious problem: misconduct that shaped the jury's understanding cannot be disproven by the verdict that resulted from it.

Courts rely on the verdict to cleanse the process.

The verdict is not independent of the misconduct. It is its product. Yet the system repeatedly treats the verdict as neutral proof that the process must have been sound.

That reversal of logic is where adjudication collapses.

This is not a hypothetical concern. It arises from a real federal criminal case. The account that follows is drawn from an actual prosecution, an actual jury verdict, and an actual post-conviction record. The misconduct described here was raised with specificity. In key instances, it was expressly acknowledged by the court before trial began. What failed was not notice. What failed was adjudication.

Rather than resolve the misconduct, the court allowed the case to proceed unchanged.

Here is what that looked like in real time.

The prosecution engaged in personal, private interaction with a juror before trial, and the court acknowledged it but failed to act.

Before trial began, a member of the prosecution team approached a seated juror, shook his hand, and expressed personal sympathy related to a traumatic event the juror had disclosed during jury selection. The juror responded positively. The interaction was brought to the court's attention.

The court acknowledged the contact. The judge asked what had occurred. The judge then asked defense counsel what he wished to do. The court acknowledged the contact and briefly questioned the juror. The inquiry, however, was limited to whether the juror believed that he could continue to serve without bias. No questions were asked regarding the nature of the interaction, the emotional context surrounding it, or whether the contact altered the juror's perception of either party.

This form of inquiry substitutes self-assessment for constitutional analysis. A juror who has experienced a personal loss and received direct acknowledgment from one party is not situated to objectively evaluate the influence of that interaction. Gratitude, sympathy, and identification are human responses, not indicators of impartiality.

By accepting the juror's assurance at face value, the court treated the appearance of neutrality as sufficient, without probing whether impartiality had, in fact, been compromised.

Later, in denying post-conviction relief, the court concluded that the incident did not warrant relief because the juror stated that he could remain fair and because the jury ultimately convicted. The court also emphasized that defense counsel had been invited to state a position at the time, treating the absence of further objection as dispositive rather than examining whether the inquiry itself had been constitutionally sufficient. An inquiry that asks whether bias exists, without examining how it may have arisen, does not safeguard impartiality, it merely records its denial.

The court never confronted the asymmetry. Had the defense initiated private contact with a juror under similar circumstances, the response would have been immediate and severe. Because the contact came from the prosecution, it was minimized.

In a pretrial proceeding shaping how the jury would understand the case, the prosecutor attributed a factual statement to the defendant that was disputed by the defendant, and the court relied on the assertion despite the absence of any identified record source.

In opposing the defenses motion for relief, the prosecutor attributed a specific factual statement to the defendant. The defendant accused the prosecutor of making the statement up. That accusation triggered a legal obligation.

The court did not require the prosecutor to identify where the statement appeared in the record. It did not order a response. It did not request a citation. Instead, in denying relief, the court stated that the allegation was "not supported by the record."

That conclusion was reached without asking the only dispositive question: where in the record did the statement appear. That was it. A single citation would have resolved the issue. The court did not require it.

This was acceptance without verification.

In a case, The defendant raised multiple allegations of prosecutorial misconduct. The governing law required the government to respond to each claim. The prosecution did not. The court did not compel a response.

In denying relief, the court repeatedly noted that the defendant had failed to establish misconduct or had offered no evidence to support the allegations.

By allowing the government not to respond, the court foreclosed the very mechanism by which the defendant could have proven the claims. The absence of proof was then cited as the reason that relief was denied.

The system created the absence and then relied on it.

Across each of these moments, the same logic governed the response.

The court did not ask whether prosecutorial misconduct shaped the jury's understanding. It asked whether the conviction could be preserved without reopening the process that produced it.

Fraud by a court officer was not disproven. It was treated as irrelevant. Verification was not required. Trust was substituted. Adjudication was displaced by preservation.

Once that substitution is made, legitimacy is no longer earned. It is assumed.

Just one question:
What would have happened if the defense had done this?

Funny how it looks and feels different when you picture the defense doing it.

The Preliminary Hearing as a Disabled Safeguard

The preliminary hearing still exists. That is the fiction.

In theory, it is the first and most basic safeguard against unfounded prosecution. It is where the government is required to show that probable cause exists for each charged offense. It is where evidence is tested early, before leverage hardens into inevitability. It is where the court is supposed to ask a simple question: does this charge belong here at all.

In practice, it no longer performs that function.

Courts do not expect preliminary hearings to screen charges. Prosecutors do not prepare them as evidentiary tests. Defendants do not experience them as adjudication. Everyone in the room understands that nothing meaningful is supposed to happen there. The hearing proceeds not as a gatekeeping mechanism, but as a formality to be cleared.

That shift is not accidental.

The preliminary hearing is disabled because a functioning preliminary hearing would expose overcharging too early. It would force prosecutors to justify theories that are later sustained only by leverage. It would require evidentiary clarity before plea pressure takes hold. It would interrupt the charging momentum that now defines the system.

So the safeguard is neutralized.

Courts allow hearsay. They lower scrutiny. They discourage adversarial testing. They treat credibility disputes as premature. They signal, implicitly and sometimes explicitly, that real challenges should wait for trial.

But trial is precisely what the system is structured to avoid as a meaningful check on charging power. Not because trials are undesirable in principle, but because a functioning preliminary

hearing would narrow charges early, limit exposure, and reduce the need for trial at all.

This is the quiet inversion. The hearing that was meant to prevent weak cases from advancing is repurposed to ensure that all cases advance.

Once charges survive this stage, however hollow the review, they gain institutional legitimacy. The case is now "real." The exposure becomes fixed. The plea differential widens. The cost of resistance multiplies. From that point forward, the merits matter less than endurance.

This is why the preliminary hearing cannot be treated as optional.

If it were functioning as designed, overcharging would stall. Statutory stretching would be exposed. Conspiracy theories without agreement would collapse. Enhancements unsupported by evidence would be cut back before they could be weaponized.

A functioning preliminary hearing might slow the process temporarily, but it would narrow the case, shorten what proceeds, and prevent trial from being driven by inflated exposure rather than proof.

Instead, the system refuses to let the safeguard operate.

Not because it is unknown.
Not because it is outdated.
But because it works.

A functioning preliminary hearing would slow the system down. It would force early confrontation. It would require judges to say no. And saying no at the front end would destabilize everything that follows.

So the safeguard remains in name while being stripped of effect.

This is not neglect. It is design.

The preliminary hearing still exists.
The preliminary hearing is still cited.
The preliminary hearing is still scheduled.

But it is no longer allowed to do its job.

That is how overcharging survives long enough to coerce pleas.
That is how statutory limits become irrelevant before adjudication ever begins.
That is how law stops screening prosecutorial power and starts accommodating it.

And that is devastating because it means that the system preserved the appearance of protection while eliminating protection itself.

When Statutes Stop Constraining Power

Statutes were designed to limit the state. They were written to define the outer boundary of criminal liability, to separate lawful conduct from criminal conduct, and to force the government to meet its burden before depriving a person of liberty. In the federal system, that function has been quietly reversed.

Statutes no longer constrain prosecutorial power. They accommodate it.

Instead of requiring charging decisions to rise to the statute, courts increasingly permit statutes to be softened, stretched, or reinterpreted to fit the charge. Elements become suggestions. Definitions become flexible. Gaps are filled by inference rather than proof. What was meant to operate as a gate, now operates as a funnel.

This inversion changes everything.

When statutes cease to function as limits, the prosecutor no longer proves a crime. The crime is constructed around the charging document. Judicial interpretation shifts from enforcement to preservation. The question is no longer whether the statute reaches the conduct, but how the charge can be sustained without disrupting the outcome.

This is not interpretation. It is accommodation.

Once this accommodation becomes routine, ordinary conduct becomes criminalizable. Money laundering no longer requires laundering. Tax evasion no longer requires evasion. Conspiracy no longer requires agreement. RICO no longer requires structure. Each statute retains its language, but loses its force. What survives is the label, not the constraint.

The disappearance of meaningful preliminary hearings completes the cycle. What once served as an early check on overreach is now treated as perfunctory or unnecessary. Challenges to sufficiency are deferred. Statutory limits are postponed. Everything is pushed downstream to trial or plea, where leverage replaces proof and the cost of resistance becomes unbearable.

At that point, the statute has already failed. Not because it was unclear, but because it was no longer allowed to do its job.

This is how law stops governing power and starts serving it.

Courts Have the Authority. They Withhold It.

The collapse of adjudication did not occur because courts were powerless. It occurred because they choose not to exercise power that they clearly possess. Understanding that choice is essential.

Courts have the authority to intervene.

They could say no, this statute does not reach that conduct.
No, conspiracy requires proof of agreement.
No, enhancements cannot replace evidence.
No, volume does not excuse constitutional shortcuts.

They have the tools. They have the precedent. They have the discretion.

What they lack is institutional will.

Reining in prosecutors would require dismissals, reversals, and public acknowledgement that charging practices have exceeded lawful bounds. It would require courts to say, explicitly, that prosecutorial behavior has destabilized adjudication itself.

That confrontation is avoided.

Instead, courts choose accommodation. Not because adjudication is impossible, but because conflict is inconvenient and embarrassing.

Adjudication is sacrificed, not to preserve survival, but to preserve institutional calm.

Why Prosecutorial Misconduct Persists

Misconduct does not persist because it is rare or difficult to identify. It persists because the system has eliminated meaningful consequences for it.

Prosecutorial misconduct persists because it is not punished.

This is not speculation. It is an observable fact.

Prosecutorial misconduct is a leading cause of overturned convictions in the United States. Yet individual prosecutors are almost never disciplined, fired, disbarred, or removed from practice. When misconduct is found, the remedy is backward-looking and procedural. A reversal. A new trial. A harmless-error ruling.

The actor remains untouched.

This is not accountability.
It is containment.

If misconduct is not punished, it repeats.

If it repeats without consequence, it escalates.

If it escalates, it becomes normalized.

That is not a moral judgment. That is institutional behavior.

Removing prosecutors who engage in misconduct would work. At a minimum, correcting them would work. Either would immediately change outcomes. Misconduct would stop in those cases. Deterrence would follow. Charging practices would tighten. This is how accountability functions everywhere else.

The fact that it does not happen here, **is the point.**

Why Judges Allow It

Judicial tolerance is not accidental. It is functional. It is the mechanism that allows the system to continue operating without confronting its own breakdown.

Judges allow this not because they are unaware of the problem, but because stopping it would destabilize outcomes that the system already relies upon.

There are three structural reasons.

First, institutional dependence. Courts rely on prosecutors to keep dockets moving. Sanctioning prosecutors creates friction. Friction slows the system. Speed is prioritized.

Second, diffusion of responsibility. Misconduct is framed as office failure, judgment error, or systemic ambiguity rather than personal wrongdoing. That framing protects individuals and prevents consequences from attaching.

Third, finality pressure. Sanctioning prosecutors invites scrutiny of past cases. That scrutiny threatens stability. Stability is treated as an institutional good.

The system quietly claims that it cannot impose accountability because it would disrupt capacity, while that very lack of accountability is what inflates the volume, overloads prosecutors and everyone else, and creates the congestion that is used to justify restraint.

So, discretion is used not to enforce standards, but to avoid consequences.

This Is Not About Immunity, It Is About Power

It is critical to be clear about what this chapter is not claiming.

This has nothing to do with prosecutorial immunity.

Immunity concerns liability after misconduct occurs. The failure here occurs long before that. The issue is whether prosecutors are constrained at the charging stage at all.

They are not.

Statutes are no longer enforced as limits on power. They are reinterpreted to accommodate the prosecutors charges. Adversarial challenge exists formally and is neutralized structurally. Proof no longer functions as a gatekeeper. Accusation does.

This is not interpretation.
It is accommodation.

It is adjudication and accountability displaced by management.

Why This Makes No Sense on Justice Terms

Even on the system's own terms, this model fails.

Allowing unchecked prosecution does not make the system safer.
It does not make prosecutions more accurate.
It does not reduce crime.
It does not serve justice.
It does not even reduce workload in the long run.

What it does do:

It produces overcrowded prisons.
It produces overworked courts.
It produces coerced pleas.
It produces unstable legitimacy.
It produces constitutional decay.

The only thing it accomplishes, is avoiding the need to say no, to prosecutors.

That is the benefit.
That is the cost.

Indigent Defense as a Structural Casualty

Indigent defense did not fail first. It failed last.

What collapsed indigent defense was not lack of effort, lack of skill, or lack of commitment. It was the redesign of risk. When prosecutorial power expanded beyond statutory limits and courts declined to reassert control, the defense function was structurally neutralized. No level of competence could overcome a system calibrated to prevent defense success.

This matters because indigent defense is routinely blamed for outcomes it never had the power to alter.

Once statutes stopped constraining charges and discretion replaced enforcement, the Sixth Amendment did not weaken. It was sidelined. The right to counsel remained intact on paper while the conditions necessary for counsel to function were systematically withdrawn in practice.

Expanded charging fundamentally changed the defense role. When prosecutors are permitted to stack charges, soften statutory elements, and threaten extreme sentencing consequences, the defense no longer operates in an adversarial system. It operates in a pressure system. The question ceases to be whether the government can prove its case. The question becomes whether the defendant can withstand the consequences of resisting.

Under those conditions, evaluating counsel's skill becomes meaningless.

Determining whether counsel is capable of handling the case they were given becomes moot when the structure of the case guarantees that success is not an available outcome. Legal acumen cannot undo statutory dilution. Advocacy cannot neutralize leverage created by charge inflation. Trial performance cannot matter where the government bears no real risk of losing.

The issue is not whether counsel is capable.
It is whether counsel is allowed to win.

That permission no longer exists.

This is where the Sixth Amendment quietly collapses. Not because counsel is absent, but because counsel's role has been reduced to procedural participation rather than outcome influence. Effective assistance of counsel presumes a system in which effectiveness can change results. Once prosecutorial authority is insulated from meaningful consequence, defense performance becomes irrelevant by design.

Courts then complete the displacement by judging defense performance in isolation, stripped of the conditions imposed by prosecutorial discretion. They ask whether counsel objected, whether counsel argued, whether counsel preserved an issue. They do not ask whether any of those actions could have mattered **once the cost of losing for the government had been structurally removed.**

The result is predictable. Defense performance becomes the explanation for outcomes that were structurally predetermined. Ineffectiveness claims fail not because counsel performed adequately, but because the system no longer allows defense competence to register as a variable.

Indigent defendants absorb the damage because they are the only participants without insulation. They cannot limit charging. They cannot moderate statutory interpretation. They cannot impose consequences on overreach. They cannot force adjudication once discretion has displaced it.

This is not a failure of defense. It is a downstream effect of prosecutorial expansion, enabled and sustained through judicial accommodation.

This is how the Sixth Amendment survives in language while disappearing as protection. This is how defense becomes symbolic rather than functional.

When the system eliminated meaningful consequences for overreach, restraint did not erode. It was intentionally eliminated.

Conspiracy as an Unchecked Weapon

Conspiracy has become one of the most powerful tools in the federal prosecutorial arsenal and not because it is well-defined, but because it is rarely constrained. Courts routinely permit conspiracy charges to proceed without requiring proof of agreement, communication, or mutual decision-making. What should be a narrowly defined offense has been allowed to be expanded into a mechanism of control.

At its core, conspiracy is a statutory crime that requires agreement. It requires at least two participants who knowingly decide to pursue a shared unlawful objective. That requirement is not ambiguous. Yet in practice, courts increasingly allow conspiracy to stand where no such agreement is shown, where no conversation is identified, and where no evidence establishes that the defendant coordinated with anyone at all.

In many cases, the only support offered is the assertion of an un-indicted co-conspirator. The designation appears in charging documents without a corresponding charge, without testimony, and without a statement establishing participation. No evidence is introduced to show that the alleged co-conspirator agreed to anything. No record demonstrates that a conspiracy, as defined by statute, ever existed.

This reversal is not minor. A person cannot be labeled a co-conspirator before conspiracy is proven. To do so is to assume the very element that the government is required to establish. Yet courts routinely accept the label as sufficient, allowing the prosecution to bypass proof by naming a relationship rather than demonstrating one.

The effect is predictable. Defendants are charged with conspiracy even when they are the only person before the court. They face enhanced penalties not because an agreement was shown, but because the charge itself carries leverage. When plea negotiations occur, conspiracy is often the charge retained, not because it best reflects the conduct, but because it carries the highest exposure and sets the sentencing floor higher than the underlying offenses.

This practice transforms conspiracy from a crime into a pressure device. It is no longer used to describe conduct. It is used to dictate outcomes.

Courts are not powerless in this process. They have the authority to require proof of agreement. They have the authority to demand evidence of communication. They have the authority to reject charges that do not describe a statutory violation. When none of those things are required, it is not because the law is unclear. It is because the court has chosen not to exercise its power.

At that point, the failure is no longer prosecutorial creativity. It is judicial accommodation. The court permits punishment to proceed without requiring the government to show that the defendant's conduct satisfies the elements of the offense. The adversarial process becomes symbolic, and statutory limits lose their force.

When courts allow people to be charged, convicted, and sentenced for conduct that has not been shown to violate a statute, legitimacy is no longer earned through adjudication. It is assumed through repetition.

That is how conspiracy became an unchecked weapon. Prosecutors did not seize this power. Courts handed it to them, in what is supposed to be an adversarial process.

The Cumulative Effect on the Sixth Amendment and Indigent Defense

Once this structure is visible, its cumulative impact becomes impossible to ignore.

Unchecked prosecution does not merely distort individual cases. It reshapes the conditions under which the Sixth Amendment is supposed to operate. Indigent defense does not fail just because defenders are unskilled or uncommitted. It fails because the system has made meaningful defense structurally impossible.

When charging expands beyond proof, defense becomes reactive. When conspiracy replaces agreement, investigation loses meaning. When enhancements replace evidence, leverage overwhelms advocacy. When courts accommodate overreach, adversarial challenge becomes symbolic.

The Sixth Amendment is not repealed. It is preserved in language while stripped of it's force. Indigent defense is not denied. It is permitted to exist without the capacity to function.

This is why correcting prosecutors works. This is why removing them works. Not because it punishes individuals, but because it restores the conditions under which adjudication can occur at all.

The system did not abandon adjudication because adjudication could not work. It abandoned adjudication because reasserting control over prosecution required confrontation that the courts chose not to have.

Now that the structure is visible, that choice is visible too.

And choices can be reversed.

What This Chapter Establishes

This chapter establishes that the collapse of adjudication was not accidental and not misunderstood.

It shows that what appears, at first, to be error, overload, or drift is in fact tolerated behavior. Repeated. Absorbed. Normalized. Protected.

The system did not lose control of charging power. It yielded to it. Oversight did not disappear. It receded. Constraint was not removed by decree. It was abandoned by practice.

What remains is not confusion about roles, but clarity about priorities. Charging decisions are allowed to outrun proof. Statutes are reshaped to accommodate outcomes. Safeguards remain visible but inert. Accountability exists formally but rarely operates.

This chapter makes one realization unavoidable:

Oh.
This isn't a misunderstanding.
This is tolerated behavior.

And once tolerated, it becomes governing.

That is how adjudication gives way without ever being renounced. That is how justice remains promised while no longer required.

Chapter 10
Criminal and Civil - Same Judiciary

Criminal and civil cases are adjudicated by the same judiciary. The same judges preside. The same ethical canons apply. The same language of fairness, integrity, and legitimacy is invoked across dockets. Courts speak of truth seeking, reliable fact-finding, and public confidence as foundational to adjudication in every context.

Yet when misconduct occurs, the system responds differently depending on whether the case is civil or criminal. The divergence is not subtle. It is structural.

That divergence cannot be explained by definition. Integrity does not change meaning across contexts. What changes is how much the system is willing to tolerate reopening an outcome once punishment has been imposed.

Integrity as a Universal Value

Courts routinely describe integrity as essential to adjudication. It is framed as the fairness of the process, the reliability of fact-finding, and the legitimacy of outcomes. These principles are not presented as aspirational ideals. They are treated as prerequisites to lawful judgment and to the authority of the judiciary itself.

Integrity is described as protecting the truth-seeking function of the court, the role of the jury, and the credibility of judicial outcomes. When courts speak of integrity, they speak in absolute terms. A process compromised by misconduct is described as unreliable. A verdict produced by an unfair process is described as illegitimate.

At this level, integrity is universal by definition. It is not contingent on the type of case or the identity of the litigant. It is described as the condition that makes adjudication possible at all.

Integrity is not described as discretionary when courts invoke it. It is not framed as conditional, contextual, or negotiable. It is presented as foundational. Without it, adjudication is said to fail. Without it, verdicts are described as unreliable. Without it, the authority of the judiciary itself is called into question.

This is not language of preference. It is language of necessity.

Integrity must be present.

When Integrity Reopens Civil Cases

In civil litigation, courts routinely reopen cases when misconduct compromises the fairness of the process. Withheld discovery, false testimony, or concealed evidence are treated as threats to adjudication itself. Relief is granted not because the outcome is proven wrong, but because the process cannot be defended.

Courts describe such judgments as unfairly procured. The concern is institutional rather than partisan. The jury was deprived of information. The fact-finding process was distorted. Confidence in the verdict is undermined.

In these cases, courts emphasize that the integrity of the process matters more than preservation of the result. Finality yields when legitimacy is at risk. The system accepts the cost of reopening because allowing a tainted judgment to stand would damage confidence in adjudication itself.

What is striking is not that courts reopen civil cases when misconduct is shown. It is how uncontroversial that decision is. There is no suggestion that reopening undermines judicial authority. No fear that legitimacy will erode. No insistence that finality must prevail.

The system understands, instinctively, that relief should be granted regardless of whether the outcome was correct, because a verdict reached through a compromised process cannot stand.

When Integrity Yields in Criminal Cases

In criminal cases, misconduct does not operate the same way it does elsewhere. Suppressed evidence, constrained defense performance, conflicts of interest, the toleration of false testimony, and the subordination of perjury may be acknowledged, but they rarely disturb the outcome. Instead, they are filtered through established practices designed to protect finality once punishment has been imposed.

This raises an unavoidable question. How can a system claim to have integrity while simultaneously accepting misconduct as a condition of stability. On the criminal side of the justice system, the ordinary meaning of words quietly changes. Integrity is said to exist even when violations are conceded. Fairness is said to be preserved even when the process is compromised. Courts then react with offense when defendants describe the system according to what it actually does, rather than how it describes itself.

The inquiry no longer centers on whether the process was compromised. It shifts to whether the defendant can clear additional hurdles placed in the way of correction. Courts ask whether prejudice can be proven, whether the outcome would have been different, whether the claim was raised at the proper moment, or whether the error can be declared harmless after the fact.

The focus moves away from the integrity of the process and toward the durability of the outcome.

Misconduct may be recognized without consequence.
A compromised process may be acknowledged without correction.

The conviction remains intact.

Integrity is not simply denied.
It is redefined.

In criminal cases, the logic is inverted. The verdict is treated as confirmation that the process must have been fair, even when the fairness of that process is directly challenged. Discretion and deference are then used to absorb the violation, allowing the outcome to stand without confronting the breach that produced it.

The defendant is asked to disprove harm that the system itself ensured could not be fully seen. Evidence was withheld. Discovery was constrained. Defense investigation was limited. And then the absence of proof is cited as proof of absence.

What would invalidate a judgment in a civil case is absorbed in a criminal one. The promise of justice does not change. The expectation of fairness does not change. The nature of the violation does not change.

Only the system's willingness to honor those commitments once a case becomes criminal. That's the change.

Integrity Defined by Discretion

The inconsistency is not definitional.
It is objective driven.

Integrity does not lose its meaning when a case becomes criminal. Courts do not suddenly misunderstand what integrity is. They continue to define it the same way they always have: fairness of process, reliability of fact-finding, legitimacy of outcomes. The understanding does not change. The moral language does not change. The standards do not change.

What changes is whether integrity is allowed to decide anything.

In criminal cases, integrity is no longer a governing principle. It becomes a consideration. It is weighed, balanced, and often discarded when enforcing it would require reopening a conviction, disturbing punishment, or destabilizing finality.

This is not confusion.
It is a choice.

Integrity is still recognized as integrity. It is simply no longer decisive. When it conflicts with outcome preservation, integrity yields. Not because it is ambiguous. Not because the violation is minor. But because correction would cost the system something it is unwilling to pay.

Integrity retains its meaning, but it loses its force.

It survives as vocabulary, not authority, in criminal cases. Courts continue to speak the language of integrity while denying it operational power. They acknowledge compromised processes without allowing that acknowledgment to carry consequences. Integrity is permitted to exist only so long as it does not require action.

This is how discretion redefines integrity without ever renaming it.

Discretion determines when integrity will matter, when it will be postponed, and when it will be absorbed. It converts a principle meant to constrain power into a variable that bends around it. What should trigger correction becomes something to be managed. What should compel remedy becomes something to be outweighed.

The system does not forget what integrity demands.
It remembers perfectly.

It simply decides when integrity will be allowed to govern and when it will be allowed only to speak.

Justice becomes conditional when integrity is no longer decisive.

Not on truth.
Not on fairness.

But on whether enforcing those things would disrupt what has already been decided.

Once integrity is allowed to be optional rather than required, justice is no longer enforced. It is rationed.

Misconduct Without Symmetry

Misconduct does not change its nature when the docket changes. An outcome that is unfairly procured does not become less unfair because the case is criminal. False testimony does not lose its corrosive effect on truth finding when the consequence is imprisonment rather than money. Damage to the integrity of the fact-finding process does not diminish once punishment has been imposed.

The promise of justice is the same.
The expectation of fairness is the same.
The injury to legitimacy is the same.

Courts describe these failures using identical language in civil and criminal cases. The values they claim to protect fairness, reliability, institutional credibility, and public confidence do not shift with the caption of the case.

What changes is not meaning.
What changes is consequence.

In civil cases, these failures justify reopening judgments, vacating verdicts, and retrying claims. In criminal cases, the same failures are absorbed. They are acknowledged, minimized, or neutralized through legal processes designed to preserve the outcome rather than to correct constitutional injury or repair a compromised adjudicative process.

The distinction is not the seriousness of the violation.
It is not the clarity of the misconduct.
It is not the harm to the adjudicative process.

The only difference is category.

One is civil.
One is criminal.

And once punishment has been imposed, correction is treated as destabilization rather than a constitutional obligation owed to the defendant.

The system does not dispute that the process was compromised. It disputes that the compromise must matter.

That is not inconsistency.
It is selective enforcement of principle. It is Discretion.

And it reveals something unavoidable. Integrity is enforced where correction is safe, and withheld where correction would threaten finality.

The promise of justice does not change.
The expectation of fairness does not change.
Only the system's willingness to honor them in a criminal case does.

Discretion as Normalized Practice

Discretion has not remained a tool within the system.

It has become the system.

What once operated as a narrow space for judgment now functions as a substitute for statute. Rules still exist. Standards are still recited. But enforcement is no longer governed primarily by law. It is governed by whether applying the law would disrupt the outcome that the system has already accepted.

This is not exaggeration. It is observable practice.

Courts now rely on discretion which absorbs misconduct rather than confronts it. They openly balance integrity against finality. They do not even hide it. They enforce identical standards differently while allowing discretion to do the work of obscuring that difference. Discretion keeps the system from having to name the choice being made. What should trigger correction is reframed as something to be managed.

Not because judges are corrupt.
Not because they are careless.

But because discretion has been normalized as the mechanism for preserving stability when law would require disruption:

Discretion has quietly replaced statute in function, if not in name.

Statutes still sit on the books. They are quoted. They are acknowledged. They still promise protection of constitutional rights, correction of misconduct, and enforcement of limits on state power. But when honoring those promises would require reopening convictions, ordering hearings, excluding evidence, or confronting prosecutorial misconduct, discretion steps in to decide that enforcement is no longer worth the cost.

This is where adjudication breaks.

Discretion allows courts to say "the rule exists" while also saying "we will not apply it here." It permits integrity to be recognized linguistically while displaced operationally. It converts unequal enforcement into something that appears technical, neutral, and inevitable. Inevitable not because it is required by law, but because discretion has become the wall that no one is able to climb. Not even other courts will climb it.

That appearance is not accidental.

Discretion is almost never described as power, even though that is precisely what it is. It is framed as judgment, restraint, professionalism. It is treated as a neutral space insulated from institutional interest. That framing shields discretion from scrutiny while allowing it to determine which principles will govern and which will quietly yield.

This is how the system avoids admitting what it is doing.

Discretion makes it possible to acknowledge compromised processes without correcting them. It allows courts to recognize violations while declining remedies. It creates a language in which responsibility can be named without consequence.

Over time, discretion stops functioning as judgment and starts functioning as insulation.

It absorbs error.
It protects outcomes.
It prevents accountability.

And once that pattern stabilizes, discretion no longer feels like choice. It feels like reality.

What begins as case-specific judgment becomes routine. What is described as restraint becomes default. Decisions disappear not because they were never made, but because they no longer have to be named.

But they still have a name.

Discretion.

What remains almost entirely unexamined is what work discretion has been doing for the system. How often it has been used to avoid enforcing statutes. How consistently it has replaced rule with preference. How thoroughly it has taught courts that law is optional when correction would be destabilizing.

Discretion did not merely soften the edges of the law.
It taught the system how to live without it.

And that is why this problem sits just beneath prosecutorial misconduct. Misconduct could not survive at scale without discretion to receive it, normalize it, and carry it forward untouched.

Once you see that, the structure becomes unmistakable.

Law still has a name.
But discretion has the force.

Different Objectives Same Judiciary

The same judiciary presides over civil and criminal cases, applies the same Constitution, and speaks in the same language of fairness, integrity, and rule of law. Yet the governing objective shifts depending on what is at stake.

In civil cases, legitimacy of the process is paramount. Error is corrected because correctness itself sustains confidence. Procedure matters. Transparency matters. Remand is routine. Reversal is not treated as failure, but as maintenance.

In criminal cases, once punishment has been imposed, the objective quietly changes. The priority becomes preservation of the outcome.

This is not accidental. It is not unconscious. It is not the result of overload or incapacity.

It is selective.

The system does not lose its ability to see unfairness when a case becomes criminal. It loses its willingness to act on it. The same courts that demand rigor, disclosure, and explanation in civil litigation tolerate assumption, silence, and deference when liberty is at stake.

That is the hypocrisy.

Finality is elevated not because it is principled, but because it is protective. It shields convictions from scrutiny, courts from confrontation, and institutions from admitting error. Integrity is honored when it stabilizes authority and subordinated when it would require correction.

The system does not lack integrity.

It allocates it.

Correction is welcomed where it is safe and resisted where it would expose fault. What is described as restraint is outcome protection. What is framed as discretion is the quiet decision to prioritize closure over truth.

The judiciary does not apply one standard imperfectly.

It applies two standards deliberately.

Justice is conditional.

Stability is not.

The hypocrisy is not that courts fail to act. It is that they act differently when acting would matter most. When one's Liberty is at stake.

What This Chapter Establishes

This chapter establishes that integrity is not applied symmetrically across the system. The same judiciary recognizes the same harms and uses the same language to describe them, yet assigns different consequences depending on whether reopening an outcome threatens punishment and finality.

The refusal to apply fairness consistently is not a limitation of law. It is a choice about which outcomes must be preserved.

Chapter 11
Once You Have Seen It

This chapter names what changes once the system is understood. The system does not become different. Participation does. Legitimacy no longer supplies the vessel through which action is taken. What fails is the assumption that engagement occurs within a structure oriented toward justice. What follows offers no solutions. It records the consequence of knowing.

When Correction Stops Being Presumed

This section marks the first rupture.

What fails is not belief in justice, but the assumption that the system is oriented toward constitutional correction.

Fairness does not surface on its own.
Error does not compel response simply because it exists.
Procedure does not activate constitutional protection by default.

These assumptions persist only so long as adjudication and justice are treated as the system's governing objectives. Once the structure is visible, that premise fails.

The system does not enforce constitutional protection because a violation has occurred. It enforces only when enforcement does not threaten outcome preservation. Procedure no longer functions as a safeguard. It functions as a sequence whose completion is treated as sufficient.

Once enforcement is no longer presumed, participation must account for what the system actually does, not what it promises.

Participation Conditioned by Discretion

Once the structure is understood, it becomes clear why ordinary participation fails. Most legal practice assumes that careful argument, legal coherence, and persistent exposure of error will eventually compel correction. That assumption is incorrect.

Error is not confronted on its merits. It is absorbed by discretion, routed through procedure, and neutralized by finality. Writing that looks for fairness to yield misunderstands the system's design. Writing that seeks full enforcement of statutory limits misunderstands it even more. Statutes are no longer governing constraints. They are materials that discretion works around.

This explains the phenomenon of occasional success. Small wins occur. Narrow relief is granted. Discrete corrections are made. These outcomes do not reflect systemic responsiveness. They reflect discretion choosing accommodation over disruption. Limited relief sustains participation without altering structure.

There are, however, moments where absorption fails.

Consider a case in which post-conviction counsel uncovers contemporaneous investigative material that exists independently of the trial record: preserved communications, third-party financial records, or agency logs generated outside the control of the prosecution. The material does not reinterpret testimony or invite competing inferences. It fixes reality. It establishes dates, locations, transactions, or events. Those facts directly contradict a factual premise necessary to sustain the conviction. The theory presented to the jury cannot coexist with the record as it actually exists. The contradiction is not analytical. It is factual.

That independence is decisive. Because the evidence was not selected, shaped, or framed by the prosecution, it does not arrive as an accusation against an actor. It arrives as a record. No office must be scrutinized. No motive assessed. No professional judgment questioned. All of which ordinarily trigger discretion.

Consider proof uncovered through post-conviction investigation showing that, on the night that the government alleged the defendant committed the charged conduct, the defendant was arrested elsewhere and held in custody. The record is contemporaneous. It is generated by a separate agency. It fixes time and location in a way that cannot be reconciled with the theory presented to the jury.

In such cases, courts often grant limited relief. A hearing is ordered. A narrow remand issues. A conviction may be vacated, or a count dismissed. Yet the relief is framed as exceptional, fact-bound, and non-precedential. The outcome is corrected, but the structure remains intact. The system concedes because it cannot absorb the proof, not because it has re-embraced adjudication.

This is not a full win. It does not recalibrate charging practices. It does not alter the law itself. It does not restore the Sixth Amendment as an enforceable guarantee. But it forces movement because discretion has lost the ability to route the problem away.

Many attorneys spend years operating inside of this system and come to be regarded, correctly, as excellent lawyers. They are skilled. They are diligent. They win more often than others. What is less commonly understood is why they win.

Their success does not come from argument alone. It comes from investigation that produces facts that the system cannot easily absorb. Work that forces confrontation rather than routing. Evidence that resists procedural containment. The system can ignore theory. It struggles to neutralize concrete, developed, external proof.

Even then, success is partial. Wins are permitted where they can be framed as exceptional rather than structural. This allows the system to concede without conceding anything that would require recalibration.

Most attorneys do not recognize this dynamic. They attribute success to skill, reputation, or legal mastery alone. Those qualities matter, but they are not decisive. What matters is whether the work presented can be safely absorbed. When it cannot, discretion shifts.

The irony is this. Many of the lawyers most capable of winning more often do not, because they still operate as though the system responds to persuasion or statutory completeness rather than pressure created by uncontainable proof. Understanding the structure does not guarantee success. But without that understanding, even excellence is constrained by rules that the system does not actually follow.

Time as Structural Control

Time is not neutral in this system. It is functional.

Delay narrows records.
Exhaustion limits challenge.
Finality converts unresolved questions into settled conclusions.

The system does not wait accidentally. Waiting produces closure without adjudication. Once this is understood, time is no longer experienced as administrative. It is recognized as one of the primary mechanisms by which outcomes are protected.

What Recognition Does Not Provide

Structural clarity does not produce leverage.

It does not guarantee relief.
It does not force accountability.
It does not undo harm.

It does not restore what was lost.

Recognition removes illusion. It does not transform the system into something responsive. Nothing in this book promises that understanding will be rewarded.

What Recognition Changes

What recognition changes is alignment.

Truth becomes something to preserve rather than something the system is expected to vindicate. Documentation becomes central, not as persuasion, but as record. Legitimacy is no longer granted automatically. It is assessed.

This is not optimism. It is realism without illusion.

The Cost of Recognition

Clarity carries cost.

Ease disappears.
Assumptions fall away.
Isolation follows.

This is not weakness. It is the predictable result of recognizing that enforcement is optional and that outcomes are protected. The cost of clarity is real. The cost of ignorance is worse.

What Cannot Be Unseen

Understanding cannot be undone.

Participation will not feel the same. Language will not function the same way. Process will no longer be confused with justice.

The reader is not told what to do next. That is intentional. Once the structure is seen, pretending otherwise is no longer possible.

Bridge to the Conclusion

What follows is not guidance. It is an accounting.

The final chapter records what the system has chosen to prioritize, what it has chosen to tolerate, and what that alignment reveals.

Once seen, that record cannot be unseen.

Chapter 12
Conclusion: What This System Has Chosen

This book began with the Sixth Amendment because it is the constitutional site where failure is most carefully managed. Not because the right is unclear. Not because its meaning is contested. But because its enforcement has been transformed into theory while its consequences remain concrete.

The Sixth Amendment survives in structure. It is recited, cited, and treated as settled law. It is taught as guarantee and referenced as assurance. Yet its operation has been severed from its form. What remains is not confusion about what the right requires, but discipline around when it will be allowed to matter.

The Sixth Amendment promises adversarial testing as a governing condition of legitimacy. It does not promise representation in name alone. Appointment was never the right. Enforcement was.

What this book has shown is not that the Sixth Amendment failed to develop. Its enforcement was deliberately rerouted away from adjudication and into mechanisms designed to preserve outcomes.

That displacement is structural.

Indigent defense reveals the failure first because it is where enforcement is least buffered and least forgiven. But indigent defense is not the origin of the problem. It is the point of exposure. The Sixth Amendment is constrained before representation begins, by choices that determine whether adversarial testing will be permitted to occur at all.

By the time counsel enters, the field has already been narrowed. Charging decisions, procedural compression, discretionary thresholds, and institutional tolerance for imbalance determine what kinds of failures will be examined and which will be absorbed. The appearance of defense failure is the downstream effect of upstream design.

Each stage of the system contributes to this result.

Discretion determines whether violations will be confronted or managed. Finality determines when inquiry must end regardless of what remains unresolved. Jurisdiction determines whether any forum must decide at all. None of these mechanisms deny the Sixth Amendment. They neutralize it. The right is permitted to exist so long as its enforcement does not interfere with settled outcomes.

Finality rules. Once a judgment is entitled to closure, enforcement becomes conditional rather than compulsory. Enforcement is invoked when it stabilizes outcomes, deferred when it threatens them, and avoided when adjudication would require disruption the system has decided not to tolerate. No one pauses to ask, who elevated finality to this position, or how it came to outrank the very rights that the system exists to enforce.

This arrangement is not sustained through ignorance. Courts understand what the Sixth Amendment requires. They describe it accurately. They articulate its purpose without confusion. What has changed is not comprehension, but response.

No court rejects the Sixth Amendment. That is not how this system operates. The right is preserved in language while its force is redirected into procedure, discretion, and deference. What disappears is not the promise, but the obligation to enforce it. Correction is what this system fears the most.

This architecture is reinforced through alignment. Discretion is extended upward and inward. Professional risk is minimized. Relationships are preserved. Non-adjudication becomes rational. Silence becomes survivable. Closure becomes proof.

The system still knows what justice is.
The system still speaks its language.
It simply no longer allows that language to govern.
What survives is not law, but Discretion.
What remains is not confusion, but alignment.

This is not a broken system.
It is a system operating exactly as it has chosen to operate.
It is operating by design.

ONE LAST THING

The phrase *Due Process* appears only once in this book.

WHAT'S SCARY IS THAT:

Most of you didn't even notice.

THAT is the point.

Neither does the system.

It was not even needed to keep the machinery moving.

Afterword

Now that you have read this book, it is worth pausing. The analysis may linger in ways that are difficult to name. I understand this feeling.

You may find yourself replaying moments that once seemed ordinary. Decisions that once felt neutral. Silences that once passed without notice. They may not look the same now. They shouldn't.

What remains is not outrage. It is something quieter. What you are seeing is clarity. A sense that what now appears familiar has been newly arranged. You recognize that the things you once tried to explain away, or tried to make sense of, no longer require explanation.

You may notice a shift in how absence feels. In how finality feels. In how discretion feels. Not because anything new has happened, but because something has been recognized.

For some readers, especially those who have lived inside of this system without its protections, that recognition may feel heavy. To all, it may bring relief. It may bring discomfort. It may bring both at once.

This book does not resolve those feelings. It only gives a place for them to exist.

You may struggle now to unsee what you have clearly seen. I know that I do.

If it lingers, something has been recognized.
So, if it lingers, let it.

About the Author
Freya D. Pearson

My work is shaped by a journey through the federal criminal justice system that forced a level of understanding that few are ever required to develop. What began as participation in the system, became a sustained study of how it actually functions once constitutional rights encounter discretion, deference, and finality.

I am a Paralegal and I hold an ABA-approved Paralegal Certificate, an Associate's Degree in Paralegal Studies, and a Bachelor of Science Degree in Law & Paralegal Studies, earned Summa Cum Laude, with a minor in Criminal Justice. My formal education provided the legal foundation. My lived navigation of the system provided the missing instruction: how law operates when enforcement is optional, and outcomes are protected.

I have experienced the federal process across trial, direct appeal, and post-conviction review, both with counsel and pro se. At each stage, I encountered the same pattern. Constitutional rights were acknowledged, but their enforcement was deferred. Claims were recognized, but the merits not adjudicated. Discretion was extended upward, while indigent defendants were required to meet impossible burdens using records shaped by the very deficiencies under review.

That experience did not produce grievance. It produced clarity. I learned that survival within the system required more than legal knowledge. It required understanding of how silence is treated as sufficiency, how absence becomes proof, and how review can legitimize failure rather than correct it. I learned how humanity is extended generously to institutions and insiders, while those without power are rendered not worthy of it.

Reclaiming the Sixth Amendment is the result of that journey. It is written by someone who was required to learn the system from the inside, not as theory, but as a consequence. I do not write to assign blame or relitigate outcomes. I write to name the structures that allow a constitutional right to remain intact in form, while its enforcement quietly disappears in practice, and to show why indigent defendants bear the cost of that design.

A Final Word

In this country that was founded on freedom, we must remind our rulers of the devastation that their enormous power of discretion can yield.

Sometimes they need to be reminded that as much as we need them for **Order**, we also need them to be **Just**.